THE HUMOR HACK

THE HUMOR HACK

Using Humor to Feel Better, Increase Resilience,
and (Yes) Enjoy Your Work

MICHAEL K. CUNDALL JR.

RESOURCE *Publications* · Eugene, Oregon

THE HUMOR HACK
Using Humor to Feel Better, Increase Resilience, and (Yes) Enjoy Your Work

Resource Publications
An Imprint of Wipf and Stock Publishers
199 W. 8th Ave., Suite 3
Eugene, OR 97401

www.wipfandstock.com

PAPERBACK ISBN: 978-1-6667-3876-6
HARDCOVER ISBN: 978-1-6667-9984-2
EBOOK ISBN: 978-1-6667-9985-9

04/26/22

To my family, friends, colleagues, teachers, and all the rest who bring smiles, humor, and mirth to our lives.

Humor is mankind's greatest blessing.

—MARK TWAIN

Contents

Preface | ix

Chapter 1: This isn't a Workbook, it's a Playbook | 1

Chapter 2: Humor as a House—An Allegory of Course | 7

Chapter 3: Humor and Health: An Overview | 14

Chapter 4: Humor Basics: Incongruity | 23

Chapter 5: Mirthful Meetings | 31

Chapter 6: Lighthearted Workspaces: Designing for Levity | 39

Chapter 7: Lead with a Joke | 48

Chapter 8: Humor Under Pressure | 60

Chapter 9: Office Humor | 69

Chapter 10: Classrooms and Teaching Spaces | 78

Chapter 11: Electronic Laughs and Digital Spaces | 87

Chapter 12: Humor and Apologies | 98

Chapter 13: He Who Laughs Lasts: Concluding Thoughts | 108

About the Author | 111

Appendix 1: More Playbook Activities | 113

Appendix 2 : Further Reading | 119

Preface

If you're reading this book, if you've only just picked it up, you've at least some interest in humor. Maybe you're worried about the same things that I am: that humor is missing from large parts of our lives; especially in our professional endeavors. That humor is crucial in times of stress and we don't rely on it as much as we should. That humor is being relegated out of our work and personal lives. That we're pushing humor experiences into a box and we only experience humor at certain times. Maybe you just want a few more laughs because you, like I, love humor. Whatever your reasons, this book can help

My name is Mike Cundall and I am a philosopher/philosophy professor. Yeah, I know what you're thinking—"*Philosophy! I had that class.*" Well, it's not half as bad as my parents' first thoughts when I told them I was majoring in philosophy. I heard the "want fries with that?" joke a good bit. Still do. But give them credit. They didn't dissuade me too much, or perhaps not enough. With your purchase (wink, wink) of this book, they can now finally tell their friends I've done something with my life. They'll say, "He wrote a book. A short book. A book about funny stuff. But hey, a book!"

How does a philosopher write a book on humor? Well, it's because I happen to study the wonderful world of humor. Yes. I get paid to study funny things. I can't complain too much. I started researching humor in graduate school during my dissertation work on autism. It seemed that persons with autism had a different appreciation of humor and laughter and if we understood that in some depth, we'd not only better understand the disorder, we'd be able to develop better ways to work with people with autism. Alas, due to a variety of circumstances, I didn't get to pursue that research.

As I wrote about humor and my job duties grew and changed, I became interested in humor and the workplace. My interest grew because nearly all of those leadership lists one comes across never once mentioned humor as a quality or characteristic of good leadership. That seemed and still seems wildly wrong. It's also a glaring omission. I began to see the huge numbers of disengaged people in the workforce—nearly 80% of workers by some accounts. It shocked me how many of us were disconnected or detached, and that it's been that way for decades. These high levels of disengagement have stayed high despite all the leadership consultancies that have sprung up in the past decade. As a result of all this I realized that humor could provide us a solution.

With all these thoughts in my head, I started thinking about how we can effectively use humor in our organizational spaces, and in our lives. The result of these thoughts and many presentations I've done over the past couple years is this book. But don't go thinking it's a typical book. I decided to write a different kind of book. I decided to write a sort of playbook that is part humor discussion, part summary of some of the academic research, and part guide to help you, the reader, learn and play around with humor in your life.

This book provides you with little strategies you can use to take what we know about humor and put it into action. You're going to "hack" your mind into getting more funny out of the world around you. I offer little exercises or play breaks throughout the text to help you practice and play around with some of the concepts you just read about. The point of this is to provide you ways to begin to apply humor in your personal and organizational life. It's only limited by how far you want to take it.

For some of the early exercises I provide some sample answers in the text. There are also further exercises in appendix one (I'm an academic so of course I need to have an appendix right?!) Don't take my answers as the necessarily right ones. They're just models. Use them, discard them, but do the exercises. There's no test at the end and no points to earn, so you don't have to worry about a grade. All the exercise sections of the text are marked with the smiling face picture you see to the left of the first "exercise." It's just a cue that helps break up the reading and provide you with a smile as you read. These exercises are there to help you interact with the book and, dare I say, play with it. If you treat this book more as an object of fun rather than a tome you need to study, you'll get more out of it. So let's get to your first chance to play.

*Exercise: Do you find it amusing
that I study humor? Why?*

To help you as you start playing around, I will give some sample answers to the "exercises" so you can get an idea of what a reasonable answer looks like or at least what my answers look like. Don't get overly worked up on giving the right answer. If you are thinking and engaging with the questions, that's pretty good.

Sample Answer: This is a bit tough to start out with because I really can't answer this question from another's perspective. I don't find it funny that I study humor. It's an area of study like any other. But I do see how other people would. *This guy's a philosopher and philosophers study deep things, important-sounding things like being and the mind-body problem. He's studying jokes. I want that job. I want to deal with funny stuff instead of the boring stuff I normally deal with. He gets paid to read about funny things and laugh! Yeah, that's hilarious to me.* Or at least that's how I imagine someone responding. If yours is different, please go with it.

So why in the world should we focus on humor? Maybe you're skeptical that any book like this can help. Why not just go watch more YouTube videos of cats knocking cups off tables? C'mon, you know what funny is; you know what makes you laugh. You don't need me to tell you what you find funny.

You're absolutely right. You are an expert on what makes you laugh. What could some ivory tower philosopher have to tell you that you don't already know? Since I don't know you, I can't tell you what you find funny. I wouldn't dare. But this book isn't about telling you what you find funny. It's about helping you get more funny out of the world. Because if you look, humor abounds.

What I promise you is that this book is designed to help you get better at humor and if you follow along, you will get better at finding ways to increase the amount of humor in your life. You're not going to find things more funny, but you will find more things funny. What will happen by reading this book is that you will up your humor game. You will be able to more effectively and artfully use humor. Your world of humor will grow. Maybe you're a huge fan of physical comedy. Perhaps at the end you'll enjoy more satire and wit. Maybe you find puns obnoxious. I daresay you'll appreciate all of them a touch more. My goal is for you to enjoy more humor and love the humor you do enjoy more deeply. I'll wager those around you will too. From family to friends to coworkers and acquaintances, humor makes things better. Humor matters. There's even a hashtag for that #humormatters. Check it out.

Exercise: When do you use humor in your life? Do you find you use it more at certain times than others?

Sample Answer: I find myself really trying to insert humor into ordinary interactions with strangers or in day-to-day customer service type situations. We're all programmed to say "not bad" when asked "How's it going?" or say "Thanks, I appreciate it." At the close of an interaction I try to use humor to shake people out of that rote almost robotic response loop we all fall into.

Humor matters! It matters a lot. Humor has all sorts of measurable benefits. It can reduce stress, improve resilience, and make us more effective and efficient in our activities. It improves our mental and physical health, and makes us more resistant to disease. Humor can make you smarter and more creative. There are mounds of research from the medical sciences, social sciences, neuroscience, and yes, even philosophy that tell us about the importance to having a good life. But there's one you already know. You know how you feel when you laugh, smile, or share a joke with a friend or colleague. You feel the warmth of mirth making those moments better. It's actually this word for the warm, fellow-feeling, 'mirth' that I used in naming my company, Mirth Management (www.mirthmanagement.co). This is no coincidence. Humans didn't develop humor for no reason. And one of the reasons it feels good is because it can be so helpful.

Andrew Carnegie once said, "Where there is little laughter, there is little success." Many people complain that their organizations and workspaces are sorely lacking in humor. Laughter is noticeably missing. That's why the absence of humor from our organizational lives is so much the worse. Laughter doesn't make you a worse employee. Mirth and levity don't make you less effective. When used right, all of these enhance our day to day lives. They make us more engaged individuals who will do that little bit extra with a smile, who will reach out and happily be at work. Humor makes us better friends, family members, and even lovers. It's a shame that we've come to see laughter and play and enjoyment as something antithetical to accomplishing our serious goals or something that's only an enjoyment. Humor, laughter, and mirth are important and necessary parts to any successful life. That's why I am writing this book. It' why I work to help people understand how to use humor effectively in their lives.

Humor serves a lot of purposes in our lives. Unfortunately that purpose and the space for humor has gotten oddly misaligned with our daily activities. It's misaligned because we've been sold a lie. Actually a lot of them. We work hard so we can play hard. We suffer the drudgery of work so we can go on vacation. We push ourselves and are serious in the pursuit of our goals. All work and no play makes Jack a dull boy, or so the saying goes. In short, there's no space for humor, enjoyment, laughter, or mirth in a world dominated by objectives, deliverables, and progress.

This is all patently, hilariously, false. There's a twisted irony lurking in these thoughts that marginalize humor and laughter. Work and play are not opposites. Serious is not the opposed to laughter in our lives. They're part of how we live effectively and efficiently in the world. If we focus too much on one, we lose the other and are less for it. I urge you to play more, to find more things funny, and to look at this world as an almost inexhaustible source of humor and laughs. I don't want you to think that you're just going to share more memes or YouTube videos. You're not going to simply imbibe more humor. You're going to make it for yourself and for others to imbibe. Your humor muscles will flex and grow.

I invite you to take your time and read this at your leisure. Keep it by your bedside, maybe in the loo, or maybe on your desk at the office for times when you need a lift. Of course, you could get three copies and place them around in strategic locations and help a philosopher out. But don't take this too seriously. Don't study it deeply, not yet. There are no grades waiting at the end of this, no additional letters you can put on your business card when you're done—though I am sure that we could come up with some. Rather than approach this as work, play with it, make no expectations of yourself as to an outcome, an improved process, or workplace made better. Even though I am sure those things will come if you find ways to bring more humor into your life. But if you follow through with this book, if you think about it here and there and throw in a little study too, you'll start to see noticeable benefits in your life.

This book is a hybrid between a workbook and primer. It's why I call it a "playbook." There are many out there that discuss how and why to use humor in your organization and I encourage you to support the other humor apologists out there. There will be a further reading section later on in the book. Whether your organization is your work, your religious group, your gym buddies, or community group, our lives within those organizational spaces can be substantially improved by humor. You know this. Let's start putting into practice.

If you're trying to introduce more humor into your life, think of it like exercising. Most of us don't start with an under 6-minute mile, a 250lb bench press, or a perfect arabesque. We have to work up to it. Humor is a skill no different than any other. It can be improved by practice and training. This playbook is part of that. You're going to have days when your jokes or wit are not well taken. It may be your fault; it may not. I have a particular story that I tell that almost always gets laughs, but one day it didn't. (You'll come across it in chapter 9). I still can't tell you why it failed when it did. But audiences are different, so not every joke or bit of humor is going to work in all cases. I have no idea why the story failed and I've thought way too much on it. But I keep telling that story and still, every time but that one, it has the desired effect.

In general, I keep looking around for more times and places where I can deploy my humor. That's the key—practice and commitment. It can be hard to inject humor, especially in places where it is largely absent. Don't be discouraged. Eventually it will get better. You will get better and more effective. But if all we accomplish is that you find a little more humor in the world, that you find a smile on your face more throughout the day, then that's a win. And make no mistake, it's a big win. It's also the perfect start for having those laughs and smiles spread. Once you see more humor and experience it, those around you will be drawn to it as well. The humor and laughter in your life will begin to increase, and that's a good thing.

If you've made it this far, then let's get to it. Let's explore humor, see some examples of humor at work, and see how together we can work to increase laughter, smiles, levity, mirth in yours and all of our lives. I imagine we'll all be the better for it.

CHAPTER 1

This isn't a Workbook, it's a Playbook

Most of the books you find on humor tend to be one of two sorts. The first is a sort of handbook or compilation of examples, where the author hopes you will be able to use to help you use more humor. *See how this was funny over here? Go try it over there.* The second kind is a deep dive into the research and theory of humor. This one arms you to the teeth with the latest research, the theory extolled by philosophers, psychologists, and comedians. But these tend to do little to tell us how to move from theory to practice. Both are good. I've a number of both on my bookshelf and enjoyed them. Writers will focus on humor and spiritual matters (*Between Heaven and Mirth*), others will focus on humor in your life (*Using Humor to Maximize Living*), while still others focus on humor use across peoples and eras (*Mirth of Nations*). Some are long (*The Humor Primer*) and some are shorter (*Jokes: Philosophical Thoughts on Laughing Matters*). Some are more like textbooks you'd find in an intro class in a college. Others are more scholarly and focus on a particular discipline. They've all strengths and weaknesses.

I thought what was missing from all of these was a book that the individual could work with and have fun with. One that provided you opportunity and space to play not only with the ideas, but with the book itself. My hope is that this book is a mix of reader, playbook, and humor lab where you get to make things up, read, explore, and have some fun.

Exercise: Make up a joke about the stuff within 5 feet of you. Don't worry if all you have is a chair and the floor beneath your feet—you're not writing for a comedy show. This joke may never meet the eyes of anyone but you.

Sample Answer: Near me right now there are two pillows. The best I got is this. Two pillows are sitting in a house while the house is on fire. The one pillow says to the other "Hey man, the house is on fire. We should leave." The other pillow responds "Holy crap! A talking pillow." This isn't a great joke and it's not even original—I heard a version of it about muffins in an oven. But at least it was a riff. If all you do is alter a knock-knock joke, or riff like I did on a joke you know, you're already far along in your humor journey. We all have to start somewhere.

I encourage you to really play around with this book. I hope that this book is your companion as you grow and build those humor muscles. We're going start with your expertise on humor and move on from there. We're going to rely on what you know and supplement it with some of the know-how that comes from good old research done by some wonderfully clever folks.

This book is designed to be played with. One of the things I constantly say, and you've picked up on, is that we need to reintroduce play into our lives. Go into any elementary school and you will see that often the most engaged and effective classrooms have good doses of play in them. The room is decked out to be fun and visually interesting. I am not saying make your office space or bedroom décor be dictated by a preschool color palette, but greige may not be the best way to go. Pay attention for opportunities to increase humor in your life. They're quite a few if you go looking.

Exercise: Find a notebook nearby, or a scrap piece of paper. Rip out a piece. Pretend you're ripping it from the book. Then crumple it up and make the contested basketball shot at the buzzer to win the game. Don't wait too long. Those precious seconds are ticking away. You're moments away from being a hero.

(In an early draft of this book I envisioned a perforated page people could just rip out. Publishers were not as enamored of the idea as I was. So we get to a little make-believe and go a different route.)

If crumpling up a perfectly good piece of paper rubs you the wrong way, then make a paper airplane from a separate piece of paper and fly it. Throw it at a friend. What was their response? Really, stop reading and do it. I'll wait.

Get in the habit of actually engaging with humor. You'll find that you see more of it around and your life and those around you will be enriched. Humor is often related to seeing things just a little differently. That page isn't just a blank page, it's a chance to doodle a funny picture, a chance to be the hero at the end of the game, or design an awesome paper airplane and see how well it does. The more you open up your world to finding funny things, by encouraging play, the more engaged you will be whether you're at work, at home, or riding the subway. Try it out. It may feel weird at first, but you'll find yourself seeing more and more opportunities for humor.

For example, I was getting a flu shot the other day and since we're in a pandemic (at the time of writing), the pharmacist asked me if I was up to date on my other shots. I had no idea and asked "What sorts of shots?" She said, "For folks over 50 we recommend the shingles vaccine." I responded, "Well, I am not over 50. But thanks for that!" I was teasing/being sarcastic which I hope my exaggerated voicing showed, and her response indicated she meant no offense (I wasn't offended) and said all the things to assure me that I really didn't look over 50. I really looked young, but she just didn't want to assume. I was simply teasing. I told her I wasn't miffed, and we had a good chuckle. It's moments like this that I cherish. I had a little fun with someone who was doing her job, and it made the process more enjoyable. There was also no need for her to feel embarrassed, so hopefully my humor allayed her worries.

If we're going to bring humor into our lives more, then perhaps another little story can show where you can begin looking and the benefits humor can bring. Again, the opportunities for humor abound. I was calling to pay a bill for one of my son's doctor visits. I made it through the touch-tone phone labyrinth and got the billing manager on the line. I don't know if you've visited a medical office recently, but they are laid out such that the office/billing manager is typically located in the center of the building surrounded by a moat of files, fax machines, printers, all far more imposing to guest and worker than the traditional cubicle walls. That girdle of technology isolating her from the rest of her colleagues. Here is our billing manager whose entire existence is dedicated to the most awesome of all things in our modern world: bills. A steady stream of insurance companies denying coverage, people disputing charges, people like yours truly who didn't pay the bill on their way out the door, adding to the paper trail she gets to deal with. Any and all the headaches that come with money and bills, sitting in an office with no windows, isolated from colleagues, make for a great working environment. It's a thankless job.

When the individual got on the line with me, you could hear her disengagement. Her entire presence was flat and lifeless. There was nothing there but a person going through the routine. I would have been more engaged if it was more of an automated system. At least I could make sarcastic comments without anyone getting angry. It was unnerving and unpleasant for both of us. It's also totally understandable.

She asked why I was calling, what the account number was (of course I didn't have it), what the date of birth of the patient was, etc. It was like talking to a computer that had given up hope. She asked me if I wanted to pay the bill in full, and I said I did. She then asked me how I wanted to pay. I told her a credit card, and then she asked which credit card I wanted to use. It was then that I saw the opportunity to change the tenor of the conversation. At that moment I had this little flash, a little impishness took hold of my brain. I ran with it and said, "Well, can I use your credit card?" And there was this silence. An almost complete dead silence. Though I swear I heard the gears in her head turning to process what this doofus had just said. And just when I thought it was going to go wrong, you could hear the smile break in her voice (we are really good at hearing levity in people's voices by the by) and she said "No you can't use *my credit card!*" I playfully responded "Are you sure, 'cause I'd really like to." And she said "no" still laughing and shocked by what had just happened. I paid the bill, exchanged the pleasantries we all do as we close a call, hung up and that was that.

The big difference, and the thing that is so amazing about humor, was the complete change in her voice and interaction with me. After my little joke—if it was that— the whole interchange was different; she was animated and engaged. I *talked* with her, and she with me. Though I never got her name, I knew that there was smile on the other end of that line, not simply a person watching the clock. We actually conversed rather than traded information—though that obviously happened too. Oh, and she got my money. It was a win win for her.

The interaction was rewarding for both of us. I'd like to think, and there's evidence to support it, that for the next few hours, her day was all the better. I'll wager her coworkers noticed it too. She may have even told them the story of the goofy guy on the phone asking to use her credit card. I'll bet her significant other heard the story too and smiled. Humor like this reverberates out into our lives like ripples on a lake. Humor like this improves our lives. I remember the incident not just because I think it's funny, but also because it was such a change in our interaction. When we began the interaction it was customer and biller. By the end, we were two people having a more enjoyable conversation. We weren't friends, but we could have been.

 Exercise: When have you used or been around a situation where you noticed humor making things better?

Sample Answer: I see kids using humor to diffuse tense situations all the time. They try to get folks to laugh and get beyond the bad feelings.

The above examples give you a good idea of how the book will go. Throughout the book I'll use examples to introduce ideas and give you an anchor point to work from. I'll also spend some time on some of the research that will help further our understanding of humor and why and how we can use it with that research in mind. I'll get you to think of times in your life when humor worked, or didn't. I want you to remember those times and save them for later. That credit card bit has had more mileage than just the doctor's office. I use it in books (wink wink) and talks and it has never failed to make the point I want it to. Humor is really important and underutilized.

As we close out this chapter I want to remind you of an important fact. In the business world, in our ordinary workdays, in our organizations we are surrounded by things we have to do. We have To-Do Lists, projects, activities. We circle back to follow up and get the low down. We don't waste time on the extraneous things like fun, laughter, and enjoyment. Work is work and fun is fun and they don't meet. This thought is fairly well-entrenched. It's also laughably false! Go ahead, laugh at it.

Worse than that, this assumption is partially responsible for why we have such high levels of disengagement in the workplace. Don't make this reading and the work involved something you have to deliver. When we're constrained by To-Do Lists, by deliverables, we lose the ability to be creative, to have fun. This is why work feels so awful. There's no space to play. Take your time and play with this book. Don't make it and any of the work inside another deliverable. Play around, it is a playbook after all.

This is the beginning of your humor exploration. Don't take it too seriously or view it as a race. It's all about having fun with the things you find funny and finding out that there are plenty of other ways you can inject levity and lightheartedness into your life. It's not the destination, it's the journey. It's also the company too. It's all those things. What's not to love about that? Get that smile started and dive right in. Maybe you remember that exercise from earlier when I asked you to rip out a page of the book?

Perhaps you were a bit worried or skeptical? The thought of ripping up a perfectly good piece of paper may not have set too well with you—I totally get it. With what you've read so far are you a bit more willing to have a go and tear out a page? If you're still a bit nervous, maybe tear off a corner flick it at the person nearest you.

 Exercise: Humor Inventory. Where do you find humor the most in life? Where would you like to see it more?

Sample Answer: I see humor the most with my family and friends. We jabber on at times, make fun of one another, and joke about our jobs. It's a sign we're good friends when we laugh and joke with one another.

CHAPTER 2

Humor as a House—An Allegory of Course

One of the questions I often get as a presenter when I talk about humor is *how do you know when and where to use humor in an effective way?* That's one of the more difficult questions to answer, especially in a straightforward fashion. One could choose to sort of summarize the research out there and try to give a thumbnail sketch, but that runs the risk of over simplifying things and that could lead to trouble. One could then go into all the detail and present the research and issues in as thorough a fashion as possible. It's doubtful anyone could accomplish that task alone, not least of all me. But more importantly we already know that it would be TLDR. That's a different sort of trouble.

 Exercise: What do you think makes funny things funny? Write down the reasons. You're likely to be wrong, but don't worry: that's the beginning of all learning.

Sample Answer: If I actually answered this, I would be giving away the chapter. Can't do that!

I want to give you the reader something more than a thumbnail but less than a dissertation. So I've done what other famous philosophers have done. I made an allegory. Yep, it's my totally shameless attempt to appear alongside

7

the greats. Before you flash back to that introduction to philosophy class fearing Plato's Cave, hear me out. I want you to think of humor as a house. Thinking of it this way will help you to understand and interpret when and how you can use humor effectively. Maybe your house has a foyer while mine has a mudroom. You may have a great room, while mine is only above average. Don't worry, good analogies are pliable. Go with what you know. If you think of where and when you can use humor as similar to a house and the various rooms in it, you'll begin to see how this allegory will help. So let's start imagining.

Pretend you're a salesperson or a new acquaintance visiting the house of someone you've just met. Perhaps you're meeting them for the first time as they open the door. As they open the door and you make your initial introductions there is space for conversation. That's the first space of the house. When you're on the front porch, there isn't much that you two share, other than the place. Humor works on shared backgrounds. That's why humor in a foreign country is often hard. The cultures are often very different. But since you're there at the doorstep, you'll have noticed some things already. Hopefully the person opening the door lives there. It would be ironic if you interrupted a burglar. Perhaps they're the same age as you. Maybe they're older, maybe younger. In any case that will tell you something about what humor you might use. The important thing to notice is that there's not much there on the surface that you might use to find common ground for humor. But there are commonalities.

Exercise: Have you ever wanted to use humor early on in meeting a person or group of people? What stopped you?

Sample Answer: Yes I have, but the things that block me are: it's a new group of folks, the meeting feels overly tense, or I'm tired. There are good reasons for refraining from humor, but from all I hear, we need more levity in our meetings. We'll get to that in chapter 5.

The important thing when you're first meeting someone or new to a place and you're looking for a way to use humor is to look for commonalities. Perhaps the weather is bad outside. Make a wry comment about the weather. One student described the heat in my former home of Louisiana as "disrespectful." I stole that as soon as I heard it. So if you recycled an old joke for that exercise in chapter 1, you're doing fine.

As a parent, when I meet other parents, many of whom I don't know, we will find ourselves griping and commiserating over the crazy, jam-packed schedules our children have and how we're driving all over the place. We may also joke that we're not sure when the last time we spoke with our spouses let alone shared quality time. Perhaps the roads in your town are filled with potholes. Maybe you're in an area where people joke that the state flower is actually an orange traffic barrel or cone. This is a favorite of people in my hometown of Cincinnati, Ohio. These are the sort of surface level commonalities that many of us share and when we don't know people all that well, if we choose to advance humor into our interactions, these are the safest topics with which to begin. I am sure there are others, but be thinking about these general, easy, shared similarities. Those are the common grounds for humor.

When you're just outside the front door, your joke about the pothole or overwrought children's schedules may have gotten a smile or even a chuckle. Perhaps they just shook their head and gave a half smile. That's a success. Even if you aren't fast friends by the end of your time on the front stoop, you haven't been asked to leave. They haven't shut the front door. Let's imagine things went well. Now you've been invited into the foyer, or the front room. Side note, at my house rarely does anyone enter into the house through the front door. We all use the garage.

If you have been invited inside, things are still a bit formal, you're still learning about this person and them about you. You're not eating supper in the kitchen, or relaxing on the back porch just yet. But when you're in that front room you've definitely created some good fellowship. This is impor-tant because humor often works best when people have a sense that they know you in some ways—a bit of positive regard. You'll also have had a couple conversations and know a bit more about that person. The humor that you use will broaden. Perhaps you're like me and a parent of that child with the overdone schedule. Are you as tired as I am? Make a joke about how you used to sleep in on the weekends, and that brunch was a thing you used to do. But now it's a far-off memory of a mythical place you're never likely to visit again. But now that you're inside start paying attention to your surroundings. Are the walls filled with artwork, family pictures, perhaps they've only just moved in and boxes are hanging about. Maybe they're knee-deep in home repairs. The more you're paying attention, the better your chances for humor will be.

Exercise: What are the things you share with the people you work with? What about your organization's space/location is something people typically talk about?

Sample Answer: I share lots of things. The air we breathe, the building we share. But we're also members of families, have work place stresses. I work on a college campus, so having students who ask you inane questions like, "when is my exam?" for classes you don't teach, is hilarious and annoying.

Of course if things go well you might be invited back for dinner. Now you've made it to the dining room. Still formal to be sure, but clearly you're liked enough to warrant such inclusion. The breaking of bread is an important step. Why do you think so many dates involve a meal? Nothing says "hey, we're interesting to one another" than watching someone shovel foodstuffs into their mouth right? But here you're going to be able to learn more and thus know more about your hosts' likes and dislikes. You'll have conversations and interactions that will make the use of humor both easier and harder. Did I say harder? Yes, I did. Just because you're sitting down to dinner and know more doesn't mean that all the things you may find funny will be shared. One of the great dangers in humor is letting that freak flag fly a little too high too early. We all have those unique things we find funny that few people share our appreciation of. Many of them are innocuous enough, but at the dining table, maybe rein it in a bit. Pay more attention to what they're saying, and what they're discussing. See where you can find humor in those things. Don't ridicule or poke fun. The more you listen at dinner, the more likely you'll be invited to the cook out and there, the humor doors can burst wide open.

So far this allegory is rather one-sided. It's focusing on how you, the new person, or the person wanting to use humor, should be thinking and proceeding. That's fine, but remember, humor often requires two or more folks. There's the audience, the people that live in that house. Pay attention to them and how they behave. In my house we don't wear shoes. That might show you I am a neat freak (I am). Maybe don't joke about things or make fun of cleanliness. It could alienate me. I of course ask our guests to take off their shoes because I am a neat freak, so I open the door a little for some light ribbing. But remember, most houses have occupants and they are the ones you're using the allegory on to find out how and when to use humor.

All allegories are incomplete, and I don't want to go through every room in the house. Surely we don't want to discuss bathroom humor right? But if you're in the family room, hanging out with the relatives and other friends, or maybe you're in the backyard helping with the grill, you will find that the humor you can use and how it's accepted will be easier. You'll have a lot more commonalities from which you can drive your use of humor. You'll get to know their sense of humor and they yours. Perhaps you make it to the point that you no longer knock and can walk right in. That's huge. As you get to know someone, as you learn more about them and them about you, you will become more comfortable in knowing when and how to use humor. You will also develop shared bits of humor, things that you laugh about together. Then you're likely in the kitchen sipping and sharing your favorite libation.

If you remember anything about the humor as a house allegory, it's the importance of paying attention to the person you've met and the environment. You're active and engaged in listening to them, making connections in your head with the aspects of their lives that you learn. It's the ultimate listening game and if you play it right, that game will get you some laughs. It will also make you look for commonalities and then ask you to find some forms of humor in those commonalities.

Wherever you are and whenever you're thinking of how and when to use humor, if you're a little confused, or uncertain, think about the humor as a house allegory. Are you in the kitchen? Are you on the back stoop? If so, the rules change—well they're more guidelines. But as you begin to use this tool, you'll become better at using humor and being aware of what you're doing. You'll start to be a more engaged and attentive user of humor. And if you're reading this book, that's partly what you're after.

A couple of little odds and ends before we wrap up this chapter. Maybe you're still a bit confused as to what is appropriate, when and where. If you're ever worried, or you get the sense that humor might not work, don't force it. A good guideline might be "When in doubt, assume you're at the front door." This will help you remember what sorts of topics are good and the ones that should be left at the front door. Also, don't try to joke and laugh about things you don't find funny. Perhaps worse than seeming unhumorous (not sure that's a word—autocorrect sure doesn't like it), is seeming inauthentic.

There is a certain joy that we have and others notice when we're fully engaged in something, whether that be humor, a project, building a house, whatever. I may not find diagramming Latin sentences across several chalk boards in a classroom a fun use of my time, but I had a Latin professor who loved it. He was, I kid you not, giddy while doing it. I was shocked at this and I kind of half asked him, half exclaimed "you really like this don't you?" He said "Hoc amo! Puto id esse magnum!" Even when I was in Latin class,

I couldn't translate that (sorry Father Ryan). That translates to "I love this stuff. I think it's great."

I probably will never be that person who bounds down the chalkboard (yes, I was in a school that had chalkboards), but I learned something important from him that day. His exuberance, his sheer delight was beautiful to behold. It took all my teenage cynicism and cast it away. The sight of a slightly overweight and balding priest literally bounding down the board getting geeked about diagramming sentences made me realize how special it was to see someone doing something they love and enjoy. It also showed me that such exuberance is a cherished part of life. As you share more with people and begin to develop that common ground, you will surely begin to have more moments like these. You'll share with them and they with you. And who knows, maybe you'll be moved to appreciate Latin grammar.

Exercise: We share a lot more in common with one another than we might first think. We just have to look. So here's a longer form exercise. Go out to a public space and look around at folks you see. Find ways in which you're similar. What are qualities that you share? What are the differences? Is there anything funny about those similarities and differences? The similarities don't have to be deep, like a love of a certain type of food. They can be rather surface level. Hey, they're wearing a shirt like me (I hope) But you'll see that if you start on the surface, you'll start to see more and more similarities. Once those are in place, the humor can grow.

Finally, what we find funny as individuals may be shared with many, a few, or none other than ourselves. The fact that more people find the Three Stooges funny than do those who love absurdist humor is no reason to prefer one over another. Your humor is yours. If you love deeply absurd jokes, as I do, if you love puns, don't place a value on the kind of humor you like as better or worse. If you like it, if it makes you laugh, then be fine with it. But know that if you're a big fan of a niche sort of fiction like historical, cyber-punk, vampire, romances, then, most people won't get those jokes related to historical, cyber-punk, vampire romances. You do have to know your audience. This why the humor as a house allegory is so helpful. It helps you to get to know that audience to be able to use humor that's appropriate. Don't rely on niche humor when your goal with the humor is to laugh with others who may not occupy that niche. There are certainly things you find funny that others share with you. It's not that they might not find your niche humor funny at some point, but they lack the background to make the humor work. You could provide it for them and who knows, they may come to appreciate that historical, cyber-punk, vampire romance joke you love. That people have different backgrounds, that we find certain things funny and others not, isn't a problem as such. It's just a truth about humor. We need to know enough about the subject matter to be able get in on the joke. But my love of absurdity is no better than my son's love of cartoons. They're both humor and when I can share those times of humor with him, I am a lucky person indeed.

 Exercise: Ever heard someone say "I guess you had to be there." when responding to someone's humor? Why do we say that? What does it tell you about how to use humor?

Sample Answer: I had a friend in high school and we used to say this to each other all the time. Whenever each of us tried to relate a funny story, we would say this to the other. It didn't matter if it was a funny story or not. We just did it to mess with one another.

CHAPTER 3

Humor and Health: An Overview

The best physicians are not just superb diagnosticians but men who understand the phenomenal energy (and therefore curative propensity) that flow out of an individual's capacity to retain an optimistic belief and attitude toward problems and human affairs in general. It is a perversion of rationalism to argue that words like 'hope' or 'faith' or 'love' or 'grace' (*and 'laughter'*) are without physiological significance. The benevolent emotions are necessary not just because they are pleasant, but because they are regenerative

—NORMAN COUSINS "THE HUMAN OPTION" (ITALICS ADDED)

In the last half-century, research into the role of humor, laughter, and the feeling associated with humor and laughter, or mirth, has blossomed. Researchers, some no longer hemmed in by the view that humor research wasn't serious work, and others who were simply interested in humor, began to explore the effects that laughter and humor have on a person's health. What researchers have found, and what is being shown more and more across subjects as diverse as psychology, counseling, medical science, neuroscience, and yes, even philosophy, is that humor and laughter are important for good health.

Exercise: Why do you think humor and laughter are important for good health?

One of the most influential researchers who helped get the broader public and the academic community to pay attention to the role humor plays relative to our health is Norman Cousins. It's the reason I begin this chapter begins with one of his quotes. That quote sums up an important issue that anyone who wants to bring humor up as an important part of the world, whether that world academia, medical sciences, or the working world. Humor is assumed to be unimportant, a frivolous thing that we don't need to pay attention to. We can't waste time on things like humor when there are much more serious problems requiring our attention. The reason for this assumption is obvious and one that is deeply rooted in our modern lives. Work and health are serious things and laughter and humor are, by definition, not serious.

Cousins, later in his life, was diagnosed with a variety of illnesses, like heart disease and a form of connective tissue disease. He began as anyone would by seeking and receiving standard medical treatment. But over time he became disillusioned with the way he was progressing. He began to worry that the atmosphere of medical care didn't promote health and recovery the way it should. This isn't too surprising, most of us don't go to the hospital or doctor's office for fun. We go when we're needing treatment. But beyond this, Cousins felt that those needed human experiences that come with love, hope, grace, and the rest were being improperly excluded.

Given his realization, he decided to take his recovery into his own hands. He began to intentionally add those uplifting experiences into his regimen and found that laughter and humor were really impactful on his recovery. He discovered that ten minutes of full laughter helped him sleep better as well as deal with pain. It's his book, "*Anatomy of an Illness as Perceived by the Patient: Reflections on Healing*" that helped place humor and laughter as important factors in helping the body restore and maintain health. As he came to understand, the benevolent, feel-good emotions, like laughter, humor, and mirth are restorative. That they feel good is an indication of the work they're doing on our overall health. In fact, their being restorative and regenerative is one of the reasons they feel good. It's the body telling us that those things are good and that we should try to promote their occurrence in our lives. While he made the study of humor and laughter's effects as somewhat more respectable, it's still not easy to be taken seriously when talking about the importance of humor in improving our lives.

Cousins' experiences led him to look for alternatives to the traditional medical care. He found that route to less helpful and less overall productive of health. He essentially began to see that if his "body" were made healthy, but his soul or mental health was the price, the reward of good health was likely bought at too high a price. He felt that he should be bringing other things into his treatment regimen. This isn't to say he avoided traditional medical care. He didn't. He just started to sense that the traditional focus on "correcting the problem" was leaving out much that we value in life. It turns out that leaving these sorts of experiences out exacerbates our problems. He wanted to reinsert those valued elements, those benevolent emotions, into his treatment and his life. Thankfully for him and us, it worked rather well because his work was and is deeply influential. But for all Cousin's work, for all of what he and later researchers has shown, there is still a skepticism about the power of humor.

For instance, when I tell people or prospective clients about what I do, that I work with organizations to help them improve engagement, customer relations, communication, and employee satisfaction by focusing on humor in the workplace, they often respond saying something like, "Yeah! That's cool. We *need* more humor in our work lives!" They instantly realize that humor is often one of the things that's in short supply within most organizations. They see the problem and they know humor and laughter can help. To borrow sales language, they recognize the problem, they agree it needs addressing.

I'll then ask them if it's cool enough to hire me. And that's when the discomfort sets in. They'll shrug, seem momentarily confused and sheepishly say "No." While it's somewhat fun to watch them struggle to make sense of the contradiction they just walked into, it's more worrisome to me because part of my living comes from working with organizations to show how humor is important to the health of both the individual and the organization. They know the problem. They see and feel it every day. They also know, like you do, that humor is an important part of our lives, a crucial part of making our days better. But they balk and hesitate, they rationalize themselves out of something they not only know they need, but also something they realize is missing. This is how powerful the assumption that work and play, that humor and seriousness as being opposites has in our lives. It's an assumption that Cousins shows directly interferes with our health and well-being.

It's the height of irony too. The first rule in sales, and anyone who tells you what to do to sell your product, says that you have to be fixing a problem. If there's no problem, or the solution doesn't seem right, then no sale. As for the problem, clearly there is one, they admit as much. They then agree that the problem needs a solution. But when I ask them to put up or shut up as it were, they balk; they grow visibly uncomfortable.

This response is particularly troubling for someone who tries to make a living showing people the power of humor. Admittedly, as a non-sales, non-business person, I probably could do more to get them to "buy" into my services. But if you understand the problem and agree with the solution, why the hesitance in investing in something we know is important to health? As a philosopher that sort of response just floors me.

To get a sense of just how deeply we believe that humor and seriousness are different let's do a little role-playing. Don't worry, no safe-words needed here. Imagine you're tasked by your organization in helping to create more employee engagement (remember employee disengagement is ridiculously high, nearly 80% by some estimates). You come across this person who suggests using humor to improve engagement. You're interested to a degree. Would you be willing to convince your boss to bring this stand-up philosopher to talk about humor, and conduct some workshops to promote humor in the workplace? Imagine giving them the fee structure? You can already hear your imaginary boss saying "You want me to spend how much so that the employees can joke and laugh around more?! We want them more engaged so they can do more work, not less." So before you even think about it, the approach is struck from the list. You decide that the latest leadership craze where people take a survey telling them which dog breed they are and how various dog breeds work well together to achieve their goals is the way to go. And sure enough, your boss, an avid dog lover, and who you later find out is actually a Frenchie and not a Dane as they insisted, agrees.

 Exercise: What are some things you've heard or seen that tell you that humor and laughter are not serious like work? I am reminded of the saying "Work hard, play hard."

Sample Answer: My students are often unprepared for humor. I'll make a joke or try to be funny in class and often they just stare at me. I have to give permission to laugh and be playful. Just as there's no crying in baseball, there's no laughing in our serious, ivory-tower education. But just because we're serious about education, doesn't mean we can't also have fun in the process. It's not an or. It's a both and.

The assumption that humor and seriousness, work and play, are opposites and necessarily interfere with one another is false. More importantly this view leads to problems we could avoid if we changed how we approach work and play respectively. This assumption also has some unfortunate, but predictable, outcomes in the realm of health and healthcare. When we study health or healthcare, the main focus is on disease or issues that impede good health. Remember, few of us go to the doctor's office for fun, regardless of what they tell you about colonoscopies. For example, if you have bad knees, as I do, then we treat the issues with the knees. I stretch more, I go to a physical therapist, I alter how I run (not much), or I medicate with steroids or anti-inflammatories—my favorite one is Vitamin-I (ibuprofen). One solution I tried was to stop using my knees altogether, but my waistline rebelled.

Whether in business or in medical care, we fix problems. Unfortunately, this focus on fixing the problem often causes us to miss the factors that promote health or ignore the situations that led us to our issues to begin with. We'll try to change things here and there in response to the problem all while ignoring that it might be how we're living that leads us to the issues. So many of our modern issues with weight could be cured by altering our sedentary ways and adopting a better diet. Changing the conditions that lead to the problem not only helps us to avoid the problem, but also alleviates worry about a solution that may be difficult or expensive. I do not look forward to the day I need to have an MRI on my knees, but I can change how I work them to make life better. Though I do miss dancing like I used to.

Since we tend to focus on problems and how to fix them, we create all sorts of things to solve the problems we have. That's one of the many promises of US industry. Build a better mousetrap and all the problems are solved. Don't worry if your food storage habits might be the source of the mice taking up residence in your pantry. Have cell phones whose screens crack too easily? Ask some material sciences folks to engineer a more robust screen. Have a problem with cancer? Get some medical science researchers together and do the cellular and molecular research to fight off that cancer. It's all in the genes. Laughter and humor aren't problems unless they're interrupting the problem-based research and the provision of solutions.

The solution that humor, mirth, laughter, and play offer us is ridiculously cheap, requires little research and development, and since everyone likes humor and knows what they find funny, it's easy to find. What if instead of buying that new-fangled mousetrap, you just stored your food better? If you eliminate the conditions that allow the problem to persist, you don't need to waste time and effort coming up with a solution. When I teach Aikido (a Japanese martial art) to folks, I often stress that the best way to avoid a punch is just not be there. And I don't mean to just get out of the way. I mean, don't put yourselves in positions where a punch might get thrown. If you want to be more engaged at work and take more joy in your life, stop accepting the belief that work and play are opposites. The sooner you get that, the sooner your life will improve.

The view that work and play are opposites, that laughter and mirth are not important parts of getting things done is deeply ingrained in our culture. It's going to take time to work ourselves out of this, but people have and people do. It's a wonder Cousins ever got his book published given the ideas he was promoting. It's not surprising that he didn't come from academia or government research. He was an editor, a humanist. He came to prominence through the back door. I am trying the front door, but that door is open, if only slightly because of the work of people like Cousins and others before me.

Thanks to Cousins' work, and the work of many others, humor is more respectable both in my home of academics, and elsewhere. There is the International Journal of Humor Studies and Studies of American Humor. There are groups like the Association for Applied and Therapeutic Humor that are dedicated to promoting the value of humor. There are also a handful of folks like me out there working as consultants. We work with individuals and organizations to help them increase the use of humor and laughter in their lives. It's not a bad time to be interested in humor and laughter. As a result of all this research there has been a lot of findings that show the power of humor and laughter to make our lives better.

From your blood to your brain, laughter and humor have discernible positive effects. Not only do humor and laughter help you get healthy, they also do well to make you more resilient to disease. That's right, regular laughter and humor in your life can make you less likely to fall ill. One of the more interesting findings out there on laughter and humor is that laughter (real or faked) and humor help increase the production of natural killer cells. Natural killer cells help our bodies in the fight against cancer as well as other pathogens. Humor and laughter also reduce the production of certain stress related factors like cytokineTh2. It does this by helping to increase the production of cytokineTh1, a type of protein that fights off invasive bacteria and parasites.

Levels of a variety of stress related hormones and chemicals are also reduced in your blood when you laugh or find things funny. Cortisol, epinephrine, and (don't worry about pronouncing this next one right) dihydrophenylacetic acid, are all factors that increase with stress. We know that increased levels of stress lead to less beneficial health outcomes. Especially when the distress is persistent in a person's life. Hence, anything that will reduce these factors will have an obvious benefit to our health.

If you thought laughter and humor were just good at creating some improvements in your blood, the tasty treat all vampires long for, you're wrong. Increased levels of humor and laughter have also been linked to the production of certain neurochemicals related to feeling good. Dopamine and serotonin levels, two neurochemicals related to affect and specifically depression, are increased by laughing and enjoying humor. So when you're laughing and enjoying humor, you're increasing the level of those neurochemicals that help us to feel better.

These findings are more apparent when you think about the evidence that clearly shows that repeated and long-term exposure to distress leads to drastically lower health outcomes. There's an excellent wonderfully funny book "*Why Zebras Don't Get Ulcers*" by Robert Sapolsky that details some of the issues that arise when we can't deal with stress in a natural way. Those factors, like epinephrine mentioned above, create negative health outcomes if they build up in our systems. Why people didn't then think "well, if repeated and long-term exposure to stress leads to health issues is true, then perhaps the opposite is true as well. I wonder what would happen to those same factors and people's health in situations where they weren't exposed to distress, but rather eustress (good stress)?"

Turns out, quite a number of positive outcomes. Eustress exposure to things like humor, laughter and the other benevolent emotions, helps our blood as well. Cousins knew this, and so do we. We know this, because, like Cousins we feel the good effects and there is a growing body of research literature that shows how helpful humor is relative to our physical and mental health. If you're interested, search Dr. Lee Berk and humor/laughter and you'll find plenty.

Humor and laughter also have important benefits for our ability to deal with stress and disease. Researchers have shown that repeated exposure to laughter and humor make the pain we feel seem less painful. That's right: laugh your way out of that sprained ankle. Well, not really, but studies have shown that patients report the discomfort from injury and or certain treatments are ameliorated with humor. This is important because these findings have been used to help develop programs for people whose treatment regimens involve difficult treatments like chemotherapy. For instance, patients who have to endure treatments that are consistently painful are asked to find ways to experience laughter and humor near in time to the treatment. People who suffer from terminal illnesses find that routine exposure to laughter and humor makes their condition seem less worrisome. And for the younger folks, humor and playful images are used in stressful areas like MRI machines. Furthermore, researchers have found that laughter that's not the result of humor is just as good as getting these effects as humorous laughter. The body doesn't seem to care how it gets its laughter fix. Just that it gets it. As a result, laughter yoga is now something you can practice. With all of this research, would it really be that bad if you added a few minutes of laughter in the morning? I try to catch a funny video or story in the mornings before I begin my work. Especially before I start my grading.

Exercise: Have you ever laughed when something hurt? Did it make it better?

My Answer: *Yes I have. Sometimes it's all I have in the moment. It's clearly a defense mechanism, but it's a pretty good one.*

Humor and laughter also have additional effects on health for those with chronic illness. Researchers found that humor and laughter made the prospects of their disease less difficult to face. Humor and laughter's effects aren't simply restricted to the patient in these cases. As people with chronic health care issues tend to have a caregiver beyond the primary medical team, research has shown that humor and laughter provide benefit to the caregiver as well. A caregiver and patient who share humor and laughs will also feel closer to one another. This closeness is important to creating and maintaining the bonds necessary for us to deal with difficulties later on. Further, when the caregiver feels less stressed, then they can provide care more readily and more effectively.

I have been a part of some research on humor and medical care which demonstrates the importance of humor in medical care. One of the more interesting findings was that humor was not only helpful for the patient, but also for the medical care professionals. Health care providers also use humor to help themselves cope, feel better at work, and relate to their patients better. As we know, humor and laughter help bring people closer together, and humor in care situations can strengthen the relationship between care provider and the cared for, thus increasing the efficacy of that relationship. If you're interested to read more on medical care and humor check out the book *Cases on Applied and Therapeutic Humor* I edited with Dr. Stephanie Kelly.

Finally, research has shown that physicians, educators, and yes, even supervisors are seen as more effective when they are perceived as funny. Since so much of health care and education relies on proper communication, it's no surprise that humor and laughter can be beneficial. When a health care provider can use humor they're not only treating the disease, they're treating the individual patient.

While the previous hasn't been an exhaustive summary of all the research out there that supports the effects on our health and well-being that humor and laughter have, it should do enough to convince you that humor and laughter are important aspects of our health. You also have one other positive indicator that humor and laughter are beneficial. They feel good and there's a reason for that.

As Cousins urges us to realize the beneficent emotions are regenerative, I want to take it a step further. We don't laugh or find things funny because it feel good. Rather it feels good to laugh and find things funny because they are, in part, regenerative. Our body gives us motivation to pursue them by making them feel good to us. Take advantage of that and for your health's sake as well as for the sake of those around you. If you're reading this book, then go ahead and add some more laughter and humor into your life. Your doctor may be the expert on treating your condition, but as I've said before, you're the expert on what makes you laugh. Exercise your expertise.

CHAPTER 4

Humor Basics: Incongruity

So what makes things funny? How does humor work? Why do academics love rhetorical questions? Answering the first two questions requires some explanation. The third one is an occupational hazard. There are three main theories out there. There's the Incongruity Theory, which is the most dominant approach and we will get more into it a little bit later. There's the elder Superiority Theory that holds we find funny things that make us feel superior to or better than the person we're laughing at. There's the Relief Theory that states that laughter is a release of pent-up mental energy of sorts. Both of these have support, but are not thought to be particularly likely explanations of what we find funny or humorous.

Exercise: It's funny 'cause it's true! Is that true? Because if it is, it better be funny.

Like it or not, we do laugh at people because we think, sometimes, that they're silly. That's the insight behind views like the Superiority Theory. Laughter is always laughter at, not with. There are ample reasons to think that humor is about making fun. The popularity of slapstick humor, like the kind seen in The Three Stooges films, is testament enough. We also have a well-known phrase "being the butt of a joke" as well as being able "to dish it out, but not take it" as evidence for how we can and often use humor to make fun. It's not a particularly pleasant aspect of our human condition. And as we all know, being laughed at, isn't fun. We could delve deeper into this theory, but that's not this book. Also, if you want to use humor more to create more engagement, to create more mirth, laughter at others is not going to get you what you want. For a budding would-be humorist, the Superiority approach is not the best. Plus, it seems that a lot of humor out there has little to do with superiority judgments. Puns don't really have superiority judgments behind them, do they?

As for the Relief Theory, the insight behind this theory is that laughter and humor are forms of release. I giggle hysterically when I get on roller coasters. They're not really funny, but I do laugh. Have you ever laughed in strange and possibly uncomfortable situations? I am sure you have. Lots of us can understand this theory when they reflect on the laughter that will often occasion embarrassment. We laugh to diffuse the tension. Some people laugh when they're going through haunted houses. Sometimes we laugh at funerals. That last one is totally appropriate by the way. I mean, the first three letters of funeral are F-U-N. It would be shame not to do what the name implies. But there's plenty of times when we laugh and there's nothing terribly funny going on. And this is IMPORTANT.

One of the biggest mistakes people make when it comes to laughter and humor is to equate laughter with humor. This is a mistake not just because it's factually wrong (which should be more than enough), but also it might lead you to think a joke is funny because someone is laughing. Someone may find your particular bit of humor offensive, but laugh because they feel uncomfortable. If you are going to be a good listener and search for the commonalities needed for humor to work like we discussed in chapter 3, then make sure you're not assuming someone thinks something is funny when in fact they're uncomfortable. If it turned out that most of the people you work with or supervise were laughing because you're the boss and not because the joke was funny, then you're not as funny as you think. Worse than that, you could be a source of increased disengagement in your organizational space.

Returning to what makes humor tick, let's look at incongruity. In the most general sense, the Incongruity Theory states that, for something to be found funny or humorous, one needs to perceive a sort of incongruity. What's an incongruity? Well that's the big question and it occupies and vexes many researchers (this author included). In the simplest and most general way of stating the idea, an incongruity is something that is unexpected, absurd, out of the ordinary, strange, or bizarre. Ok, that wasn't simple. I would have gone on, but you can check out www.thesaurus.com if you want to find other synonyms for incongruity and make the list longer.

Exercise: What's something that's incongruous that you've recently experienced? Was it funny?

Sample Answer: The things I have been noticing a lot lately is when people say things like "I always sometimes do that." "That's mostly true." Since I am a philosopher trained to pay attention to language use, those statements kill me. If it's always, then it can't be sometimes. Something is either true or false. It's not somewhat true. That's like being somewhat a virgin.

The Incongruity Theory is the dominant theory used in modern research to explain humorous things. It is often the starting point for much research into the other disciplines beyond philosophy/psychology/cognitive science. For example, current neuroscience indicates that the areas that support higher-level conceptual thought, are involved in humor processing. That we see areas of the brain involved in higher level cognition and conceptual thought involved in humor behavior supports Incongruity Theory's claim that humor is a conceptually based activity that involves incongruity recognition.

So now you have a sense of what makes humor work. It's not a thorough explanation but that's not needed. We've a rough and ready idea, so let's use it. It would be more helpful to do a sort of analysis of certain forms of humor, jokes, and show how the Incongruity Theory can be applied. But before we launch into some analysis of the humor examples, particularly jokes, a warning is needed. Analysis of any joke or bit of humor generally, if not nearly always, makes the jokes not funny. A quote from E.B. White is clear on this, in a humorous, Incongruity Theory supporting way. "Explaining a joke is like dissecting a frog. You understand it better but the frog dies in the process."[1] The incongruity is to be found in comparing the feeling one has at the end of the joke analysis to death. I hope that's not the case below, but you'll likely find many jokes less funny for the analysis. One bonus of this sort of analysis is that it will help you as you try to come up with more humor on your own. I have found that I now appreciate the wit behind humor when I go about analyzing it.

It would do well to do a little more unpacking of terms like incongruity, absurdity, unexpected, and bizarre. Basically the kernel of the idea is that you experience something that does not fit easily within the particular context. To use an example from the movie *Friday*, there's a scene where

---

1. This quote does come, in part, from E.B. White, but his wife was also instrumental in creating this idea. More appropriately the idea should be attributed to the couple and the quote as such, like many quotes that become sayings, is likely a distillation from several tellings and retellings of the idea.

we enter into a local bodega (a corner store) in a largely African American community and are met with a sign that proudly proclaims that the store is "Black Owned." As the camera pans down, an Asian man rises from below the counter. This juxtaposition of the Asian man, dressed in what can be seen as a sort of inner-city uniform, coming from under the counter, supports the idea that he's the owner, but the sign that proclaims the establishment is black owned. What's a person to think? The dissonance this causes, the mismatch of what we see and what we're told and thus expect is a perfect example of ideas or objects that are incongruous with one another. One would have expected the store to be run by a black person—that's what the sign says—but the scene implies it's not.

This example also helps us to see the "unexpected" nature of the incongruous. The presentation of the sign primes us to think the store is owned, not by an Asian man, but a black person. Good comedy works to create expectations and then frustrate or play with them in such ways as to get the audience to find something funny or humorous. If you want to find humor, look for ways that things don't seem to fit together. Perhaps you fancy some jumbo shrimp?

Bizarre or absurd as types of incongruity are a bit more difficult to describe as they are, well, bizarre, but they are definitely further refinements, or subsets of the incongruous. Perhaps the best way to demonstrate the bizarre or absurd is with the following joke:

> How many surrealists does it take to change a lightbulb?
> Purple fish!

This little joke is pretty good at being absurd. Who besides someone in a Monty Python sketch would use a fish to change a lightbulb?! The answer of purple fish is not relevant at all to the question. Did the punchline fail to add in the number of purple fish needed? Even if one is familiar with the "lightbulb" form of joke, this particular one works because the answer supplied is a non-answer. Just as the surrealists would have liked. Hopefully you followed that. Explaining the absurd is a bit. . .absurd. It's difficult to try to make sense of nonsense as the famous author and logician Lewis Carroll put to good use. But then that's part of what humor can allow us to do. It helps us deal in a lighthearted way with nonsense. I tend to choose that over heavy drinking.

Let's continue using this approach of relying on jokes to clarify the Incongruity Theory; it's a time-honored tradition in humor research. A fair warning is needed, as jokes are but a small slice of the humor pie. There is much more that is funny than can be covered by jokes, but the Incongruity Theory holds that any form of humor is going to have some incongruity that's necessary for us to experience humor or mirth. But as a tool for explicating humor theories, jokes are compact, easily digestible, and thus make for useful examples.

Exercise: Think of a joke you know. What's the incongruity lurking in there?

Sample Answer: I am not going to give you a joke here. I need them all for myself. Plus, where's the fun in you not wracking your brain for some forgotten funny joke?

One of simplest forms of humor in young children can be found when they actively do something contrary to expectation or norm. For instance, my children loved to take nursery rhymes that they knew well and then not say the expected words at some point. My son used to change the last word of the first line of the famous "Twinkle, Twinkle, Little Star" rhyme. "Twinkle, twinkle little star how I wonder what you. . .rooster!" The substituted word would always change, but it was typically a noun of some sort and often an animal. In a sense, he was answering the question of the rhyme. He was telling us what the star was—even if it was a silly answer. He would giggle with sheer delight. For some, this sort of play with language shows that real incongruity based humor has taken root.

Certainly, children laugh and giggle prior to their use of language (laughter shows up in babies before language after all), but this active playing with language and expectations is a mature form of humor, even if it's seen as immature to the more advanced humor connoisseurs we all find ourselves to be. The noun substitution works in a way other word types likely wouldn't. Substituting an article like "the" instead of a noun would be too weird, too incongruous. And that's a little lesson. The incongruities can't be too out there or else the reaction will be confusion, not mirth. You'd get funny strange rather than funny ha-ha. One of the other ways in which the substitution is incongruous is that the child is now violating the rhyme structure. These kids are far smarter than we give them credit for.

How is this word play an incongruity? As I noted above, the child is playing around with the expectation of the well-known lyric and substituting their own words. They are not only playing with the rhyming but also the word type. It's a double joke! Clearly they understand expectation and then are using the unexpected presence of the new word to create humor. This is textbook Incongruity Theory. But this also shows how deeply cognitive the act is.

Exercise: Look around you and see if you can do something unexpected with something nearby.

Let's look at one joke that is almost totally absurd. Full disclosure, I love this joke. It makes me smile every time I come across it. This joke comes from esteemed humor researcher Victor Raskin.

What is the difference between a parrot? (this joke makes the grammar check in Word unhappy)

None.

The right side is exactly the same as the left, especially the left.

If you can make sense of this joke, you're way better than I. The whole joke is layered with absurdities. It's more a Zen koan or riddle than a joke. There's a reason some delight in riddles like they do to humor. They're tickling the same mental funny bone. But let's get back to the joke.

The initial question is nonsensical. You don't ask about the difference between a single thing; comparison require two things. The response of "none" both increases and diminishes your perplexity. The answer is in a real sense spot-on. It recognizes that you can't find a difference between a thing and itself so there can be no difference. Again, the question is nonsense. But then the coda of the joke, in attempting to explain the answer muddies the conceptual space. The listener has to figure out how one side can be "exactly" like the other, and "especially" so at that. The term 'especially' seems to make the compared items very dissimilar. This joke would have found itself quite at home in some of Lewis Carroll's works. It's just a chain of absurdities, one seemingly more so than the next. There's nothing more to get than the fact that it's absurd.

Now that you've read a bit about incongruity, try to make a joke or a witty comment on some oddity in the world. Try it out on a friend to see if it goes anywhere. Don't worry if it doesn't. It's all about the practice. This has been a heavy bit of reading, and possibly less fun than you'd have liked. So take a break and think about some more things you find funny and locate the incongruity. Make it a game. For every incongruity you find, give yourself a dollar. Or send me one. I'd of course prefer the latter ;-).

Carrying on with our discussion of humor and incongruity, let's focus on "getting" a joke. Think about what's required for you to "get" a joke. You need to know something about it. If I told you a joke where Etruscans were the main actors, you might not find it funny.

How many Etruscans does it take to change a lightbulb?

None, they were dead before electricity was invented.

High comedy this isn't. It barely qualifies as a joke. If you know nothing of the Etruscans you couldn't possibly make sense of it. To get whatever may be going on in this poorly formed joke, you need to know that Etruscans were an ancient civilization in Italy that was conquered by the Romans early on in the Roman Empire's history. Hence they were an ancient group and had never experienced a lightbulb. Like I needed to explain that.

Incongruity, humor and jokes don't just work for the imbiber of the humor. As we talked about in the prior chapter, humor is going to work best when we share some of the same ideas. For any two people to share a joke, it's important that they share a certain conceptual or knowledge base. If you're not an English speaker knock-knock jokes will go over your head. You need to know English to get the jokes. The lightbulb joke about the surrealists works because the audience knows a little something about what a surrealist is and then uses that knowledge to make sense of the absurd response. It also helps if they know that the "how many X does it take to change a lightbulb" is a traditional joke set up. Needing a shared set of ideas is also one of the reasons that humor doesn't usually cross cultures. The *Friday* bit about black owned-might not work as effectively in say mainland China, or Tasmania. Humor typically requires more of a shared cultural and cognitive background than other forms of entertainment. So it's really important to see where the commonalities lie and when you're in that house of humor, you're paying attention.

Why does this support the Incongruity Theory? Because this obvious fact about humor shows how much, cognitively speaking, is required of us when we experience and enjoy humor. It's not like a piece of music. Bach can please someone with no knowledge of classical music or instruments though trained musicians may find more to appreciate than the lay listener. A beautiful piece of sculpture or statuary can do the same. This isn't to say that those forms of art are not complex, it's just to highlight that humor is of a different sort of experience; one that requires knowledge, expectation, and belief to typically be experienced as such. Incongruity needs cognition, belief, and expectation to work. Without it, it isn't much. Even our vernacular "Get it?" question, indicates that one has to understand the ideas involved to find humor.

One final thing about creating humor. There is nothing quite as bad as humor that feels forced. Humor works and feels better when it comes up spontaneously. Forced humor can actually make our environment feel contrived, or as my students like to say "cringey." One of the things that restricts us from finding humor is working under constraints, deadlines, and the demands to produce deliverables. When we're overly guided, overly desirous of achieving a certain outcome like humor, the less good humor will be found. Since we're laboring under the assumption that humor and seriousness, work and play are opposites, we're going to have difficulty in finding humor or paying attention for those incongruities. In addition, too much pressure to be funny, to make humor happen, will tamp down the effects we're looking for. So be careful and judicious.

If you're thinking of running out and joking about every little incongruity you come upon, hold up a moment. One of the ideas I stress the most is that you should lay the groundwork for humor. It's not that you want to turn everything into a comedy club, you don't. You don't want your office or backyard as to seen only as a fun zone. You want to be a zone in which fun and lightheartedness, the fellowship of mirth, are appreciated and welcomed. If we really are to find and use humor, we need to be open to its possibility. We need to make sure that the people we work with know it's not only tolerated, but encouraged. If we do this, then we increase the likelihood that the humor we do find is spontaneous and authentic.

Exercise: Increasing Incongruities

Take the most basic or dull thing in your house, like a sock or the mop. Find something odd about it. Can you make a joke about that? Find more things that are day-to-day and find odd things about them. The more you do this, the better you'll get. I once made students try to make a joke about things in their backpacks. One kid came up with a great joke about a thermos. He had five minutes. I, and all the other students, were impressed. I was impressed enough that I remember it many years later. Check the appendix for a little story about this particular joke.

Sample Answer: *I tried very hard to make a joke about or find an incongruity lurikng in door handles. I am still working on it. Maybe some inspiration will hit me before I publish this book. Probably not. But I keep at it. I'll find something.*

CHAPTER 5

Mirthful Meetings

Humorist Dave Barry has a wonderful eye for describing the oddities and incongruities of life. He is equal parts cynic, satirist, and humanist. Though maybe the only difference in the first two is that the latter laughs at our lives while the former laments. Dave Barry describes what many of us who've had to sit through the innumerable meetings that should have been an email already know.

> If you had to identify, in one word, the reason why the human race has not achieved, and never will achieve, its full potential, that word would be 'meetings.'

My other favorite line about meetings from the wonderful DeMotivator line of posters shows four hands each grasping the other's wrists with the caption "Meetings: None of us is as dumb as all of us." Meetings get a bad rap and often deservedly so. But without meetings, how would the many TV office comedies would have ever existed? Oh the humanity! In truth, meetings can be, without question, one of the most excruciating part of our organizational lives, but they don't have to be. The meeting fatigue many of us feel because of the pandemic or because we have to deal with too many doesn't make meetings more attractive either. But there are ways to improve your meetings. As you may have guessed, many of these improvements rely on humor to achieve an improved meeting space.

Exercise: Are your meetings fun? Could they be made to be more fun? If so what you could do to add in some levity?

Sample Answer: *I used to ask people tell me funny stories that they heard before meetings. It wasn't always a laugh-out-loud thing, but as we did it more and more, things did get more relaxed in our meetings and they ran better as a result.*

If you're a manager and you have to run meetings, you're the one setting the tone. You are the leader that people look to for guidance, energy, and enthusiasm. If you want to make meetings more interesting and less tedious, then start the meeting with a lighter tone. If possible, ask people how they are, or ask them to share something that is personal, funny, or interesting. Just make sure that what you're doing is making space for something other than the deliverables, strategies, or policies you're to be discussing in the meeting. Don't put it on the agenda, but do put it in the meeting. You're setting an important environmental cue. You're indicating that it's not all about the deliverables, action items, or bloody agendas.

As the person leading the meeting, do your best to make space for levity. The space needn't be filled with examples that are clearly humor. You're not a comic in a comedy club. Humor can be present or absent and the decision to invite humor and laughter or have them wait is yours, and that's the point. You want to create a space where the members of the meeting aren't reduced to only what they contribute to the goals and objectives of the company. You're creating space for other things to occur than simply the meeting and the agenda. You'll see them as more than an employee and they'll begin to see you as more than someone who views them as an employee.

There's a name we have for people that reduce us to simply being the parts of the company's goals or their title: bosses. We've enough bosses. We need the other sort of person: leaders. People who see us as more than the role we play, are people we call, and rightfully so, leaders. Leaders see the *person* who does the job, while bosses see the jobs the person does. This is a crucial change in focus. And one, if you're paying attention, you should work to inject into your organizational space whether you're a manager or employee or both.

It would help to understand this distinction better by borrowing some ideas from moral philosophy. You had to know that I was going to smuggle in some philosophy. There's a concept in moral philosophy, stemming from the work of the famous philosopher Immanuel Kant, which highlights why I'm suggesting that you should focus on the individuals as something beyond what they do for the company. Philosophers have used the words 'means' and 'ends' as a framework to discuss ethics for centuries. If you've heard the phrase "The ends justify the means" you know a little bit about what we're discussing. These ideas of means and ends are important if we think about the difference between a boss and a leader. If you always approach the people you work with in a way that focuses only on how and what they do for the company, how they contribute to it and nothing more, you are treating them as a mean. That is, they're simply a tool to accomplish something and that something is defined by the company not the person/individual. This focus only on what the person does in the limited role in which we see them drastically alters how we treat them. We *use* tools. We *cooperate* with people. Bosses see people only insofar as they contribute to the company or their respective job. In a saddening and real sense, they treat people as tools, not people. It's shortsighted and leads to distance and division. It also happens to be morally suspect.

A different and morally appropriate way to view people is as ends in themselves, or individuals with a host of desires, talents, and abilities. When you see someone as more than what they do, you open up not only your appreciation of them (and doesn't a person who's appreciated ultimately do more and better?) but also them of you. The widening of this appreciation builds a richer relationship. Richer relationships give more humor.

Kant argued that it's wrong to treat people as means. If Kant's correct, then a boss that only focuses on what people do rather than who they are is wrong. The individuals you work with, or whom you supervise, are more than what they do. As a supervisor, you're more than what you do for the organization. All people are deserving of being treated as ends, not means. If all a boss sees in a person, or someone that works with them, is a tool to accomplish something, they fail to consider what makes them individuals. The extreme outcome of this focus on individuals as means is slavery. One reduces a whole person to their work and ignores them as people. While work is an important and meaningful part of our lives, it isn't the end all be all of life. We are more than that. We are friends, family, and partners. We each have our own desires. Some of us love to cook and to eat. Some of us love exercise, while others can think of nothing more desirable than to hike to an isolated spot and read or stare at the clouds. Others of us write books on humor. When we treat people as ends, we value them beyond the limited ways in which we know them. We may not know much about them beyond their role, but by acknowledging that their role is only a part of their identity, we're showing we value them as individuals, as ends. This broadened appreciation makes it harder to simply use them as means to our or the company's goals.

Exercise: Name five things you really love. Family can be one of them. Don't worry, you're not selfish if you think of five things that aren't family.

Sample Answer: *I love learning new things. I love University of Kentucky basketball (I went to undergrad there). I also love my family. I love to swing dance.*

Maybe you're not a supervisor or a leader. Maybe you're someone who exists in an organization that doesn't have much of a hierarchy: sometimes called a "flat" organization. Maybe you're one of the supervised. How does this apply to you, or to anyone that isn't in a leadership role (and that's most of us really)? How does seeing people as ends, as whole individuals with aspects beyond what they do help you overall? How does this moral philosophy help us to use more humor? Why have you run three rhetorical questions in a row? Now four!!

If you take the time to focus on people as individuals who possess talents and traits beyond what they do in their role as a supervisor, worker, leader, athlete, student, child, or whatever, you're going to open to seeing more things. Remember, being able to see more about the world helps us to see more humor too. There will be more opportunity to see how this person can add value. Maybe they like to design and could supply interesting graphics to the company email that no one reads. Maybe they're someone who loves playing around in spreadsheets and is great at data management. I know I could use someone to help me there. Once you start opening up how you view someone, the possibilities for meaningful engagement increase. As do the possibilities to find areas of common ground that can lead to laughs.

It's also the case that, as you begin to look at the person as an end and see them more holistically, you're going to be able to rely on the humor as a house allegory. You're paying more attention and see more about them. You may find you share a common interest or hobby. Maybe you both have long commutes into work. Those are now places where you can find room to make jokes and share funny things about those commonalities. The more you see the person as an end, the more chances for humor will arise, and the more you will find that your relationship is strengthened. You may not become best buddies, but at least you won't simply be workplace acquaintances.

Exercise: Take a few moments, pick two or three people you have solidified, role-based relationships with, and ask yourself what else you know about them beyond the way you typically know them. If you're stumped, you probably need to have a chat with them. I need to do this with my kids. (See, I can learn too.)

There is another benefit to seeing people as ends. Humor needs incongruities to flourish. Since it's important that you look for incongruities, when you learn more about the others around you and thus see more in the world, you're going to have more opportunities to notice incongruities and play with them. This will lead to increased camaraderie. When we share laughs, when we share humor, when we see beyond the limiting roles we assign to people our world is enriched. Seeing people simply as what they do in the limited areas in which you experience them limits the richness of your world and theirs. Think of how much richer your life would be if you spent a few moments finding out more about the people you live and work with. I am sure such things would not only bring an increase of humor and laughs, but also joy. Leadership doesn't always mean that you solved the next crisis or created the next best program. It also resides in the importance of acts by reaching out to those around you and treating them as ends and encouraging that level of interaction.

As you work to develop these richer views of folks, you will find that humor flourishes in the spaces where things aren't overly regimented—where you see people strictly as means. When you ask people about their days, about something, anything, outside of work it relaxes the atmosphere. Levity begins to appear. So reach out to your folks and find out a little bit more about them. Not all will engage, but many more than you may expect will. If you do this, meetings will begin to cease being objects of ridicule and will become more engaging. If you sow the seeds of levity, laughter will bloom. And please remember, you don't need to be the one leading the meeting to do this. Humor needn't just be used to broach our organizational/social divides. You could ask your boss the same questions. You could ask your friends, coworkers, or colleagues. It's equal opportunity.

Exercise: Find a way to begin a meeting that invites people to share something. Ask folks to share a hobby they have. If you're hard-pressed to come up with something on your own, do a little digital sleuthing for Ice-Breakers. You could ask folks to share the worst Dad-Joke they've ever heard, but be prepared to share one of your own.

So now you've done a bit to make getting the meeting started a little less onerous. You're taking some time to loosen the administrative tie. So what do you do during the meeting to bring a little fun into it? There are a couple of little tricks you can use, and you don't need to be the one running the meeting to do it.

Lots of people doodle during meetings. I do it, students in my classes do it, and I'll bet you've seen it in some the meetings you've attended. Do you want to admit you do it too? Sure you do. No shame in it. In the handouts that I give when I do leadership training, give talks, and the like, I have one side with the relevant content while the other side has a playful nod to all the things we do in meetings. I leave a space for doodles, a space for notes to friends (though most folks just text each other now) and a few other spots. Rather than fight these tendencies, I work with them. I give them space to be. At the very least the folks get the wink and a nod I give to what we all know happens in meetings.

Another way to make meetings more engaging is to know that people's attention ebbs and flows. After about ten minutes you'll begin to see your first lull. Of course, if you're really good at meetings you may be done before the first lull, but then folks will complain that why have the meeting to begin with? So if you're doing a presentation, make sure you put into the presentation things that will help you keep the audience engaged or cause them to reengage.

If the heart of humor is incongruity, then throw in a picture on a slide that doesn't fit. Maybe add a misspelled word and ask if anyone caught it. Are you an agenda person? Find a way to insert a clever message into the agenda and see if anyone catches it. There are any number of things we can do to manage our audience, whether we're in a meeting, presenting to a room, teaching a class, or wherever. Knowing some tricks you can deploy at a moment's notice will make you more effective.

I teach philosophy so I have to be extra attentive to folks' ebbing attention. As a teacher I will do my best to make sure that I am doing something every ten to fifteen minutes to reengage. Often times I rely on a trick comics use called a callback. A callback is a joke or remark that references something that happened earlier in the same setting. For a comic it's something they said earlier in their set. For a meeting, it's possibly a playful remark about something earlier on, or better still something someone else shared earlier on. Referring to something someone said earlier shows you're paying attention to them and that you value their input. For me as a teacher it's to refer to something we've already covered, typically that day, though sometimes I refer to content from earlier classes.

Why use a callback? Because if the audience follows it, it means they've been paying attention too. Don't discourage callbacks from your audience either. If your audience is following your presentation and gets your callback, that means they're doing more than paying attention—they're drawing relations between the ideas you're discussing. If they make their own clever callbacks (sometimes called "smart-aleck remarks"), that's even better. If they don't get the joke or wise-acre remark then they haven't been as engaged as they needed to have been. As you may have guessed, I am a devotee of callbacks.

When I was a kid, I was the class clown and as I grew up I tended to use this technique more and more. My mom would often complain to me that "no one likes a class clown." In general I have found that not to be true. What people don't like is that a class clown dominates and takes center stage. Humor and clever remarks work best when they punctuate our lives. When they break up the monotony that most meetings succumb to. So go ahead and find ways to drop little incongruities into your meetings. They're going to help you keep folks engaged. Don't be afraid to be creative. Look for those clever interrelations and find ways to draw attention to them.

If you want to literally see a masterful use of incongruities to help people remain focused, watch a Delta Airlines pre-fight safety video. Search *Delta Safety Video Funny* on YouTube. If you find the one with the cat playing the piano, you're on the right track. The folks who designed and shot these series of videos found all sorts of clever and funny ways to make the audience pay attention. They know that most people tune out in these announcements and even more so if they come in video form. And most passengers think that once they've heard or seen it once, they don't need to pay attention again. Instead of fighting this, the people who made that video took advantage of humor and incongruity to invite people to remain engages, and it worked. Create discontinuities in the film and people will be drawn in. They'll want to double check and this will keep them engaged and listening to the important information needs to be learned. They stay for the humor and in staying learn those important safety lessons.

Another way to create some avenues for fun in a meeting is to bury little messages into your agenda. Perhaps you've heard of Rickrolling? Google it. I used to have to send out regular emails to several hundred students. It was tough to get them to pay attention. They have a lot on their plates and they get more than their share of mass emails. What I would do is bury little puzzles or games. I once thought burying an obscure song lyric was a good idea, but Google made it far too easy to find. Still, at least I got some answers.

Whatever it is that you do, make sure you're invested in it. My insertion of content in the emails that was specific to me (I often told a little story about my week) helped me build a rapport with my students. It allowed them to get to know me as something more than a compiler and distributor of information, and they had fun while reading. I heard tale of an insurance company where the email always ended with a pun. Lots of folks looked forward to the email because of the pun, regardless of how "bad" they might have been. Some people love puns that are so bad they have to go to the punitentiary. They like *pun*ishment.

Meetings and company missives don't have to be boring or annoying. Often they're not fun and some meetings may be more serious than others and hence humor isn't warranted. But those meetings are not the ones we dread. We dread and make fun of the regular day-to-day meeting, the meeting that could have been an email, or the meeting that should not have been. Those are the types of activities that the shows like *The Office* and comics like *Dilbert* rely upon to make their jokes. You can avoid having your meetings being the object of ridicule and dread if you start adding some levity.

 Exercise. Name some light-hearted ways, just one or two, you could try to add to your next meeting? Try this for more than a couple meetings. Go for 10. If you make it to eight, you're great.

CHAPTER 6

Lighthearted Workspaces: Designing for Levity

At the end of chapter four I suggested that canned humor, or humor that felt too forced is detrimental to having a more lighthearted workspace. It also happens to make humor work less well in general. If you want to increase humor, don't make it a company policy directive. An example of this sort of "forced levity" can be seen in sit-com *Brooklyn 99,* (episode 4, season 4) where the captain, wonderfully played by actor Andre Braugher, attempts to get folks to improve their moods with forced laughter and smiling. As he instructs folks to smile, no one gives a real smile. When he demonstrates a "forced" laugh, it comes off as maniacal and not funny. It's a funny bit that is also uncomfortable. If you don't want to jump over to YouTube to check out a clip, just remember that time when a teacher, parent, or adult tried to appear "with it" by coopting language or jokes that they don't get. It's rarely good and usually super-cringeworthy. My sons love to point out that my "meme-game" is woefully inadequate and the memes I use are boomer memes.

If my kids will make fun of me for not getting their jokes, or I don't share the same humor as my students do, maybe this whole "open up and see people beyond their particular role relative to us" is going to be next impossible. Maybe we're all stuck in our social stations. Maybe we think we can't use humor outside of certain areas where we know the folks as friends and certainly not in environments where formality and propriety reign. I am happy to report that the situation is not all that dire. There are well-understood ways to help humor come out. That's essentially what this chapter is about. How can we augment the various spaces in our lives, yes even the most formal, both the physical and digital environments, to encourage humor and levity? How can we lighten up those spaces? As I tell my students when dealing with bureaucracy, the key is pleasant persistence.

Exercise: Do an internet search for Peter's Laws. These are helpful.

So, let's start off this chapter with some pleasantries and a promise that we will persist even when the smiles and lol's aren't immediately present. This chapter is about prep-work: sowing the seeds of levity and mirth. We're going to be talking about those little things one can do—the easy small steps you can take to create an environment where laughter and humor aren't just tolerated, they're encouraged. One of the first things you can do is realize that the goal of what we're doing in this chapter is not actual lol's. What we're really trying to do is invite playfulness. We want smiles, or small chuckles. We're not looking laughs that get people doubled over (though those are good at times too). We want restrictions to be minor and the space for playfulness to appear. Once this space and the folks within in it feel relaxed enough, the smiles and laughs will follow. Sow the seeds of levity and laughter will follow.

Exercise: What's some easy, low-risk way you could introduce some low-level levity into your space? Don't think big here. Is the addition of a smiling face somewhere on your desk a good start? Try having an old-fashioned cartoon of the day calendar physically on your desk. It will invite people to read it and interact. Look around your space, see where people are more relaxed and think about what's going on there?

There are many ways you could create levity and mirth. So don't get too worried about finding *the* right way. Instead of immediately going into examples let's start with a story about how important play, novelty, and enjoyment are to success.

For years the only real vegetable peeler on the market was the basic metal one. It was nothing more than thin metal formed to hold a blade that swiveled. I worked with these when I was a saucier. It's pretty much the definition of workaday. In fact, the handle side was great for deseeding cucumbers—it scooped out those seeds quite nicely. The problem was the uncomfortable handle. But again, there weren't many options and it did the job. Professional kitchens can be very set in their ways so that peeler was pretty much the only thing out there. That remained true until the company Oxo, who remade the vegetable peeler using a design by Sam Farber, stepped into the marketplace. That design was so groundbreaking that in 1994 it was added as a permanent fixture in the Museum of Modern Art. Yes, the humble vegetable peeler graces the halls of one of the most famous museums in the world. If you smiled at that, don't worry. That's a pretty striking incongruity.

One of the challenges Oxo faced was that no one believed that anyone was interested in a fancy vegetable peeler, even if it wasn't expensive. The other challenge was to design a peeler that was useful for people who had issues with the smaller handle size of the traditional peeler. As the design moved ahead, the issue of grip was considered, and the product designers went through hundreds of versions. Here's where play becomes really important.

As prototypes were given to folks testers began to notice that, even though people were at first skeptical of the design, their hands and fingers would stop on the rubber fins on the handles. These fins were inspired by the old bicycle grips on bikes that had the same fins. They would begin to *play* with the fins. They'd run a finger or thumb across them. But they would spend more time using it than other prototypes because of the fins. These additional touches were critically important to having the consumer enjoy the product. Not only did the fins improve the overall handle design by being part of a larger, more user-friendly handle design, they also invited the user to play because of their novelty. This extra element where the user literally played around with the item and simply felt the fins and how they acted made the product all the more interesting, made the person want to explore it, to hold it, and this led to sales.

This little tactile invitation to play, of having the fingers stop and mess around made the overall experience of the item all the better. That little change, a change rooted in novelty (incongruity) and play helped make people like it more. This in turn made it sell in ways that astounded.

Exercise: Have you ever been impressed with a playful product or experience? What was it that you enjoyed about it? Write it down now. Take a few minutes and think about how it made you feel. What are your memories like when you recall it? Is there something in your organization like the vegetable peeler that could use a reboot? How would you do it?

What this little story tells us is that novelty and play are important especially if you want to get someone's interest. You need to invite the mind to play around, even if at a sensory level. Why do you think many grade school classrooms are so brightly colored? The space is part of the learning, not simply a place where it happens. Once this happens, once we're even slightly engaged in this playful way, we will expend more energy and effort to continue to play. This also fits well with the importance of incongruity we talked about earlier. Those fins were incongruous with prior experience of kitchen utensils, indeed of most utensils. That inconsistency with other kitchen utensils was a starting point only, and a crucial one at that. The novelty draws you in, makes you want to explore more. The functionality keeps you there. Incongruity to the rescue!

So this is our first direction. If you want people to be engaged, to become more present in their activities at the moment, find ways to introduce something different. Low-level changes will help you in this. Don't just change a wall color to change it, make the change direct toward something. If you want people to be more creative maybe have some rotating art present in the office. Invite the staff to choose the pieces for the next month or so. Or if you've artists among you, maybe think of showcasing their work. Take a moment in a meeting to recognize these other aspects to people. Ask the artist of the month why they do what they do, what inspires them and why they continue with it. These activities won't show up on the "progress report," but they will ultimately make those reports better and more robust. Further, don't do ask people to engage and share just because you want to "boost" engagement, or make people feel better just to get better work. Do it because it's valuable and enriching to do so. Again, see them as ends, as people. This change in focus and appreciation will help enrich everyone's life. It will make the organizational space better for all those involved.

Here are some more practicable things you could do. You could ask people in your group what their creative outlet is, or what they do for fun. You could ask them about a time they were inspired, or some great family story. Whatever the "ice-breaker" is, just make sure no one is too rote in their response. Furthermore, you don't need to be a boss or supervisor to do this. You just need to express and interest in them as a person. When you start looking at people as more than what they do in the ways you know them, the richer and more enjoyable the world becomes. When Danielle from down the hall mentions her hobby of painting, ask her what inspires her, why she does it. Would she be willing to share some with the people in the office? Be sincere. When you show this level of interest in the person, whether you're a boss or a coworker, you're going to widen your awareness. If Danielle is uncomfortable, go only as far as you think, or perhaps just a touch further. We've been trained to make our work lives as separate and not to bring in anything from outside because it's a distraction. Don't believe that. It's just another way we've stripped the enjoyment from work. It will take some time and dedication to get this sort of sharing to feel less awkward. But it will be worth it.

Creativity, engagement, and all the things we tend to lament as missing, will start to come back if you work at it; if you start small with these lower level changes. Think of the challenge to see people as more than their job as a small part of an overall workplace reforestation project. What you're trying to do is plant more fun. The primary species you're replanting are laugh trees with leaves of levity, smile branches, humor bushes, and mirth vines. Did I push that analogy too far? Yeah, but hey, it's my book. You're working to rebuild the ecosystem that has been clear-cut of fun and enjoyment. Start slowly, but keep your eyes on the forest and the trees about you. If you start making these changes you'll see improvement in other areas like creativity.

Creativity blooms when influences from different, typically unrelated areas come together. The other thing this approach, this interest in the person beyond their role in the organization creates is that they become valued for more than just what they do in the organization. Recall what I said earlier in this chapter, you need to see the people in your organization as more than just what they do for the organization. When people can bring in an aspect of their life outside the organization and be valued because of that as well, they will be all more appreciative. Writers in sit-coms will do this all the time. They will find a way to fold some interesting fact about the actor into the character they play. It usually leads to a more robust character.

So, what else could you do to help sow some levity? Maybe flip an office sign upside down. Many people have been pranked when friends change the content of a family picture that has hung on a particular wall for years and the pranked never notices. Maybe tell folks you've hidden a work-related Easter egg in the office somewhere and getting it will help you at the next staff meeting or some such thing. Make it fun, make it a challenge. Those are the beginning steps in creating a culture of levity and mirth. These initial steps are going to be crucial in what sort of culture you create.

 Exercise: What three small things could you change in and about your organization that might lead to some smiles? Write them down. Commit to doing one or two and see what happens.

One of the gags I always wanted to try in my mass emails to my students was to write some nonsense or bury a secret message but do it in white font. When you choose the white font a computer screen doesn't show it. The only way that someone could see it would be to do a "select all" function and then highlight the hidden text. I never got around to it. Maybe you could have a try and let me know how it goes.

One of the other important parts about making levity present is to show how you do it. My students always felt comfortable approaching me because I made sure to remove obstacles. I typically go by Dr. Mike, rather than Professor Cundall or Dr. Cundall. I even tell students that when they graduate they are perfectly welcome to call me Mike. These small nods towards informality are important, as they help students develop a picture of me that shows that I am more than just a professor. I also tried to begin any mass emails with some little story about my life outside of the office. I often, in telling students that I am originally from Cincinnati, Ohio and then playfully tease the students from Charlotte, North Carolina, that it isn't the "real" Queen City. Both Charlotte and Cincinnati have the nickname "Queen City." I would also playfully tease basketball fans here in North Carolina because I am a University of Kentucky graduate. These sorts of small additions go a long way towards building a picture of me and what I am that goes beyond simply my role. It invites connections and a richer picture of who I am. Again, I am more than what I do for the organization. When we add these details and more importantly look for them what we end up with is far more dynamic interaction and one that is genuinely more engaging.

There are other ways to get people to see that levity is a part of the office and, that growth, change, and challenge are valued. No practicing medical professional goes long without having to attend continuing education events. It's part of their professional development. I didn't do too well in chemistry in high school, and I can imagine that what little I did know is now horribly out of date. A few moments on the interwebs will show that one of the things we are often advised to do if we wish to stay an attractive employee or worker is to continually educate ourselves. One source said that I need to spend at least five hours a week reading new material. Hence, one of the best things we could do for those we work with is to find ways to create the opportunity to allow people, when on organizational time, the resources to further educate themselves. Maybe we can't spare five full hours, but maybe we could say that for every three hours of training a person engages in, they're allowed one hour of self-directed education or some such thing. Ask the employee to be a more active part of their growth and development. Ask for engagement. What you'll get may surprise you.

Meetings aren't just face-to-face anymore. Our survival depends on having more ways to meet! Virtual meetings, or conference calls happened, but their use exploded given the pandemic. As a result, we've all tried various ways to remain engaged in the electronic medium that is rife with distractions. There's a clever game people will sometimes use on conference calls to help keep distractions to a minimum. It's a variation on an improv game/technique called "Yes, and. . ." which I will talk more about later. One person begins with an imaginary object and then throws it to another person. The key is for the catcher to catch a different imagined object than was thrown. In either case, the point is to play around with what could be thrown and caught. One clever person said they had just caught the drift of the other person. Make sure you go at least two rounds. One round will often allow people to try and stay aloof, and that's not what you want.

One thing I would like to end this session on revolves around the idea of the brainstorming session. If you ever want to increase creativity in your organization, please don't have a brainstorming session. Those are goal directed and focused. Creativity doesn't like too many constraints. My suggestion is to encourage people to make jokes about something in your job. Maybe have them write a workplace limerick, or haiku. Encourage a play session around the areas you want to see creativity in. Don't set any goals or constraints. You may not get an earth-shattering idea at the end, but the folks will have those ideas tumbling around in their brain and in a day or two, you'll find some pretty creative responses. You'll get more and useful ideas that you would a brainstorming session. It will also be the case that the ideas won't stop at the end of the session. You'll get ideas for weeks.

Humorous Retreats

One of the now overwrought ways organizations try to develop engagement and employee appreciation is through retreats and leadership training. It was actually my exposure to all these formats that got me so interested in humor and its importance to engagement and leadership. Many of the things you see in leadership training involves games. Teams are formed, small arenas of competition are created, to encourage people to get both physically and mentally active. If you want to have a more meaningful retreat, make sure that among all that you do, there is time for fun, connection building, and engagement with topics that are not directly related to work or projects. Free folks up from the deliverables they are so used to delivering.

I am fairly certain I know why retreats exist. We get out of our offices, away from the distractions that come with a typical workday and are "free" to do more. I've even run a few retreats, but more often than not it feels like the retreat is just work in a new location. The sales brochure should say, "Come to this year's work retreat. All the work, plus more, but in a brand-new beige meeting room! Rubber chicken optional." If you winced or even chuckled at this description, you may be suffering from a case of prolonged exposure to bad retreats. Call your local humorist to see what treatments are right for you. Don't worry, the condition isn't fatal, though it's widespread.

One of the first things to remember is that if all you're doing with the retreat is doing work in a new place, you're missing the point. The general idea of a retreat is to move away from the everyday spaces and routines that can stifle creativity and engagement. We retreat to recover, reorient, and start anew. If all you're doing is taking some time to make up all the work for the upcoming term and then planning how you're going to be doing all that work, then why waste the time moving? We could have all been done with this new project earlier if we didn't have to travel. I could have packed a lunch.

If the idea of the retreat is to get away from the everyday and encourage creativity, then don't just do work. Give folks a chance to explore. Start with something simple. Maybe ask people to write down the one thing they'd love to get rid of in their jobs. Don't allow them to say other people, or work. Don't promise anything will come of it, but you, as a manager might be able to finds ways to deal with those things and make their work better. There will be some funny ones, so go ahead and read them out so as to share the laugh. If you notice there's a theme in what people want to get rid of, that's telling in and of itself. Don't out anyone or put anyone on the spot.

Exercise: Describe some of the best work retreats you had. Describe some of the worst. Are there any similarities?

Sample Answer: *I ran a retreat that began rather badly. A coworker had received a bad review and was still hostile over it. As the workshop went on and we were out of the office and the issues that constrained us there, the chilliness began to thaw. Ultimately the retreat opened up and we all learned a lot. It became one of the best ones I've ever been a part of. Being away and then consumed with activities, non-work related activities, helped us move beyond what had been ailing us at the office. It also bled over to the office and the chill didn't return even after we were back to the old grind.*

Provide some honest avenues where people can learn a new skill and let the folks decide on some of those new things to learn. So much of what we learn in college training programs is out of date so fast, that we get to feeling overwhelmed. This is especially important when it comes to technology and programs. If you're going to try out a new digital meeting space, maybe pilot it at the retreat. Create a digital scavenger hunt. When you encourage people to learn and expand, and you place a value on it, people will begin to feel more valued and they'll take up that skill more readily.

Try to break up your retreat into situations where there are clearly avenues to play and enjoy, and more work-oriented activities to try. When you reach out and show people that you value them and encourage play, you're really showing how important they are as an individual to your organizational space. Be careful to exploit situations where there is overlap. Invite someone to give a talk on something they do during a lunch break (aside from eating of course). Perhaps the author of a book on using humor in workspaces is available? Above all, don't simply make the retreat work done a few doors down, or in a nearby town. That's not a retreat. That's a change of scenery.

Levity and playfulness won't come all at once. If your organizational space is staid and buttoned up, the work may be slow going. If you're with a group where people are already friendly, the work may progress more quickly. Some days will be rousing successes and others will test your patience and creativity. But if you've read this far you already believe it's work worth doing. Be prepared to not get exactly what you want in all cases. But think of all the people you could recruit. Form your own little band of merriment. Start a Charge of the Lighthearted Brigade. People will join up more quickly than you may anticipate.

CHAPTER 7

Lead with a Joke

Leadership, leadership, leadership. It's all about leadership these days. The sheer number of leadership companies, programs, coaches, and team-building programs out there is dizzying. What's more, with the high levels of disengagement in the workforce right now (upwards of 70%, some say nearly 80%, of the global workforce is disengaged), it seems that all this leadership isn't getting us what we truly want from our organizations. As an educator the main refrain I heard from university leaders was that we were creating leaders. So nice for the leaders to produce more leaders. We were training the next generation of leaders, of difference makers, of change agents. In honors, where I spent a lot of my time, this was almost assumed true. We encouraged students to step into leadership roles and take on ever increasing leadership roles. We created programs for leadership training. Everything was leadership, leadership, leadership. Let me tell you, when a philosopher hears leadership being touted everywhere, it's a sure sign that something's amiss. If everything is leadership, then nothing is. It's like 'it is what it is.' It's true of everything, informative of nothing.

Exercise: Can you recall having a humorous leader? What was funny about them? Were they effective?

Sample Answer: *I've done enough of these. You get the idea. You don't want to hear more about me. In truth, I wish I could look over your shoulder and see how you answer these questions.*

When we clamor that leadership is the answer to all our problems, we're setting ourselves for disappointment. Worse, we're setting up unrealistic expectations not just on our students or the people we work with, but also on anyone who wants to be a leader. If you go online and look at all the traits you see included in the various leadership lists, no one could ever be all those things. No one should ever want to. Not only would it be impossible, it would be awful. The other problem with all these lists is that they all lack an important quality, one we all recognize as important to have. If you guessed that trait was humor, you're right on. Humor is notoriously absent on most of those lists. That's both surprising and sad.

Enough of the grumpy philosopher bit. I've made my skeptical point. It's time to do something about it. Why is humor important for leadership? Don't rely on just my view. Listen to what Dwight D. Eisenhower said. "A sense of humor is part of the art of leadership, of getting along with people, of getting things done." If leaders want to promote effective organizational environments, promote spaces that people want to be a part of, create a workforce that is engaged, they would do well to add some humor into their work.

As a leader, you need to lead with a joke. Leaders guide, direct, set the tone, and project a microcosm of the organization they lead. You're not trying to make every part of the workplace a space for laughs. Nor are you pushing the idea that your organization is simply one that has laughs all the time. You are trying to show people that the parts of us that use laughter, humor, that recognize incongruity, that enjoy a smile and chuckle with a friend are just as important as that deadline. If you can make moves towards those ends, you'll not only be doing something, you will be doing something important as a leader.

Exercise: Write down ten or more of the top traits you think are important for being an effective leader. Don't do an internet search just yet. Take a moment and think about what YOU think is important. Maybe say why you find them important. Once you've done that, cruise the Interwebs and see what other folks have come up with. I bet your list and any of the ones you find will have some significant overlap. See, you need to trust yourself.

In my searches of the Internet and my own thinking on the issue of leadership, I've come to see that a good sense of humor is crucial for leadership. Not only is being seen as having a sense of humor and being funny—those are not necessarily the same thing—valued in our modern world, it's also the case that if one is seen as lacking a sense of humor, that's not something we can fix, nor is it something we desire. My wife was attracted to me largely because of my sense of humor. It certainly wasn't my graduate student income. The dancing probably helped. Of course now she just rolls her eyes at me when I try to be funny.

I don't want to take too much time on this topic of humor and leadership. Dissertations could be written on the subject. If you're interested, I would encourage you to write that dissertation. I'd read it. So let's take a few traits that good leaders have. I didn't just go to one site to compile this clearly exhaustive and exhausting list. I went to at least three. I may have even visited five. Clearly this is research of the highest level.

1. Responsive
2. Intelligent
3. Humility
4. Confidence
5. Authenticity/Honesty
6. Strong Communicator
7. Empathy
8. Creativity/Problem Solving

Humor is going to be present in all of the above. For some, like intelligence, it's much easier to see how humor fits in, for others, like humility perhaps, it's less clear. But humor is or rather can be there. What I am going to do is work for a paragraph or two, not much more than that, describing how humor is related to the traits in the above list. The exercise at the end of the chapter is to then take a couple of the traits that I missed, and you found, and think about them in the same ways that I did. How can those things you find important but I missed, have humor be a part of them? How can you then take what you found and then add it to your leadership toolbox? Send me some of your thoughts. I'd love to hear them.

Responsiveness

Starting with this one may not be putting my best foot forward. Intelligence and creativity would be far better and easier to work with. But if I led with only the easy ones, where's the fun and challenge in that? The main idea with responsiveness and leadership must involve the leader figuring out what response is appropriate and then the best way to implement those responses. If you think about the importance that incongruity plays in humor, then the relation between humor and responsiveness is clear.

People who can see incongruities who seek them out, who are attuned to and paying attention for them are going to notice more than others. They're working and looking for things in the world. They're paying attention. That's crucial. When you're not attentively engaged, important things pass you by. Opening your mind to the variety of ways that things can relate to one another, some obviously and others less so, helps you as a leader be more aware. The first step on being responsive is noticing that there is something that requires your attention. You have to recognize. You can't respond to something you don't notice. If using humor makes us cognitively more flexible and aware, then we can respond more quickly and thereby be overall more responsive.

This flexibility has other benefits as well. If you're used to solving problems and addressing issues in typical patterns, you may be unable to appreciate a novel way to respond to an issue. With responsiveness, it's not just that you see a problem and respond to it. Part of responsiveness is crafting the correct response. Often there are a number of possible and effective solutions to any issue that arises. Humor, and the cognitive flexibility it creates, is going to help you see more and more creative ways to respond the issues that arise. The essence of most humor lies in the fact that some new way of seeing the world—a way that was unexpected or different. When you use humor you're finding new ways to respond to things, and this will provide a richer mental space from which you can respond to the variety of situations you will encounter.

Intelligence

The relationship of intelligence to humor is much easier to describe. One of the hallmarks of intelligence, of being smart, is to be able to recognize patterns. Some of those MENSA tests that used to make their rounds on the Internet rely on the recognition of patterns. Some of those patterns are numerical, spatial, verbal, etc. Incongruity recognition is directly related to pattern recognition. To recognize something as incongruous, you have to know a pattern, have an expectation that's violated. For something not to fit, it has to not fit in somewhere. If pattern recognition is important to intelligence, so is the recognition of violations of those patterns. That's exactly what incongruity is—a violation and in the case of humor, often a benign violation. Interestingly, comedy writers know this too. They often use the rule of three to help move their jokes along. The first and second instances help set the pattern, while the third instance allows the incongruity to blossom. When I was teaching dance (yes I, as a philosopher, know how to dance—there's always more to folks) I was told that when you do a dance move in a show, you need to do it three times, but that four times and the audience gets bored. It seemed to work.

There's something else less obvious that shows how humor and intelligence are related and it's related to, (surprise!) play. One of the ways humans, and many other mammals learn is through play. Think about how much more effective things have been when you had fun while learning. I may have mentioned that I dreaded chemistry in high school. I barely passed. But if I had found a way to make the learning of the concepts and such fun, I would have done so much better. Play makes all the work that goes into learning seem a lot less arduous (we'll talk about this more later). When our work has elements of fun, we accomplish the tasks more efficiently and effectively.

The playful intellect enjoys finding patterns and the incongruities within those patterns. Intelligence isn't just about having the knowledge; it's about enjoying the process of getting the knowledge. The playful intellect delights in its learning, but also finds ways to make the learning, when it can be arduous, playful. Someone who enjoys learning and someone who knows the value of play and humor to learning is not only a good model for those they lead, but they also help those they lead learn more and themselves become more engaged learners.

One final thing. Years ago when I was in one of my first philosophy classes, my advisor said to me that "Philosophy is the playground of the mind." I can't say that all the time I've spent in my studies in undergrad and grad school was like being on the playground. Well, it kind of was if you think of Heidegger as a big philosophical bully. But I can always reflect that it is fun to do the work that I do and even when it's tough, it's still rewarding.

Humility

Humble leaders are good to be around. They are approachable, they listen, and they engage. I can't tell you how off putting it is to know that the person in charge of your area is unapproachable. Leaders who occupy mythical places "at the top" who are less approachable can do a disservice to their organizations and the people with whom they interact. They may try to have lunch and listen sessions, but the more they create these events to relate, the more it reinforces how they are, in fact, unapproachable.

One of the ways that humor makes us approachable is that, when we share something that tickles us, that hits our funny bone, we are opening up ourselves to those we share it with. One of the examples I often use is that if we were at a party, and I was a friend of a friend of a friend, and we just happened to be in the same groups chatting away and you found me funny, would you be more or less likely to go have a cup of coffee, or hang out again in the future? Most people find that one a no brainer. When we share a sense of humor, or even when we see someone enjoying something funny, it humanizes them and makes them more approachable. That a leader can laugh shows that they are like us in important respects. I don't always find the same things funny that other people do, but I appreciate that they find things funny. Imagine appreciating your boss as something beyond their signature on a paycheck.

Exercise: If you've ever had a humorless leader, how was that experience? Would you go back?

Another way that humor can help us to be humble is in being able to laugh at ourselves. We all make mistakes, we all have goof ups. The ability to laugh at our foibles, the ability to see the humor in some of the odd things that we do, humanizes us. Having the ability to laugh at oneself, to not be so worried that everything has to be perfect makes those around us relax and work at their projects without the specter of a bosses' glare looming in the background. If you are able to poke fun at yourself, this not only shows that you too are human, but also that you are self-aware.

Quote break: "a man must not be too thin-skinned or a self-important prig." Judge Learned Hand—on a case related to libel by humor.

More importantly, often having a sense of humor, shows that you can take a joke and, that you understand that a lighthearted approach is helpful. One of the worst things you can be seen as is lacking a sense of humor as the above quote so nicely lays out. If you make fun of others but cannot tolerate being the object of some good-natured ribbing (taking the piss, giving the business), then this shows us a character flaw. It's sometimes hard for me when my kids make fun of me or beat me to a quip, but when they have, when they've been quick to the quip, I am quite proud of them. Of course my sense of super-dadness wears off a bit, but so much the worse for being super-dad. I'd much rather them feel comfortable enough to approach me and make jokes. I get to enjoy their growth.

Confidence

To be seen as funny, as being capable of using humor well, is generally a good thing. We tend to like and regard well people who use humor. On the face of it, being funny doesn't seem to relate to self-confidence does it? If you list the adjectives to describe a confident person would humor be in the top five? Try it. Think of a few words you use to describe a confident person. But hear me out. Confident people are often good storytellers, and jokes are little stories in a way. Maybe you feel as if you're humor doesn't connect or work with others. Try not to let that impede you too much. Even the best comedians have to stubbornly believe in themselves sometimes: believe their material is good. You may, at first, have to do that. But if you believe your stuff is funny, then you've made the first step towards self-confidence—belief.

Humor, the effective use of it, and the ability to share it with others is important for confidence. When you use humor as a leader you're sharing a lot about who you are. You're giving people a snapshot of a part of who you are that is not something we are typically exposed to in more professional environments. Sharing a joke is inviting someone to be closer to you, to get to know you in ways that are different and more intimate that we typically see in our day-to-day organizational lives. Anyone willing to take that risk has a certain level of confidence in themselves or else they wouldn't do it. They're willing to take that risk. They're also confident enough to invite you to be closer to them. These are subtle but important ways good leaders can connect with those around them.

Sharing humor with others also shows that you're willing to relate to people in this different way. You feel strong enough and have the desire to reach out to people and share with them. Not only is it an emotional connection, but it's a cognitive one as well. When I experience really creative humor it makes me happy, but it also challenges me to see things in these new and different ways. These interactions help us build the connections we have to one another—to strengthen our social cohesion. This increases trust and camaraderie. Someone with whom we have these experiences seems more confident to us and, reciprocally, us to them. Reach out, take the risk, and share things you find funny. The more you do it, the better you'll get and the more confident you'll feel and the more confident you'll seem to others.

Authenticity/Integrity

The notion of authenticity is quite the thing right now. It's such a cool-sounding word. Who wouldn't want to be around someone who's authentic? We love authentic styles of food, and castigate the non-authentic. Say it out loud. Au-then-tic-ity. So important. I don't want to work with someone who's inauthentic. So it's quite reasonable that we would want to work with an authentic leader. But a warning first. If authenticity is being talked about everywhere, that's your first indication, just like leadership, that it's become jargon and is losing or already lost its real meaning. Regardless, there is something to authenticity or it wouldn't have grabbed our attention. So how does humor relate to authenticity?

Effective and engaging leaders are authentic, they don't try and hide things. They're open and inviting. Humor is one of those important ways to invite people to become closer to one another. When a leader shares their sense of humor you get an insight into something beyond their organizational persona. If you happen to find that same sort of humor, it's like bonding over liking the same sort of drink. Leaders who honestly share humor with those around them, that take the risk of inviting people to see some of what they find funny risk some, but the reward is great. You will have a lot of folks identify more with you and in more important ways than just being the boss.

It's hard to hide what you find funny. When I share a joke with you, or a meme I find funny, it's quite revealing. It's like revealing to the person you just started dating that hobby you keep hidden for fear of judgment. Take puns. Some people love them, and others hate them. There's very little in-between on the issue. I happen to love good ones, clever ones, spontaneous ones, and tolerate the bad ones.

Strong Communicator

One of the more difficult things to accomplish with humor is to get across the idea that you're trying to be funny. Unless you're in a comedy club or watching a video you know is supposed to be funny, much of humor is communicating that intentionality. Researchers have many ways to describe how we signal that we said or are doing is humorous, but the problem is quite simple. How do we indicate that the words or actions we're using mean something different than what they might seem to mean on their face? Some of the ability to be good at humor is related to storytelling. If you're good at telling jokes, you're probably using techniques of good storytelling. Good storytellers know how keep an audience engaged, provide just enough information so as to maintain attention, but neither lose the audience in too many details, nor show too much and then they don't have to pay attention.

Comedians also have ways to indicate they're trying for humor. They can exaggerate their language or make wild gesticulations. They literally give a wink and a nod, or perhaps a sly side-eye. Double-takes are also helpful. But regardless, you have to find ways to let your audience know the humor is there. When I start the conversation, "Hey, did you hear the one about. . .?" most folks will recognize this as a joke. Unfortunately we don't carry, "I'm joking now" signs with us, but we do use humor daily, so if we pay attention we can practice the sorts of things we do typically do to indicate humor. In a pinch, emoji's are helpful.

When I teach my classes people almost always assume that philosophy is serious. Modern college education is serious work. There are grades darn it! It's often hard to let students know when I'm using humor because they're not open to it. They're trying to learn what's needed for the test and can't be bothered with the goofy musings of the professor. They don't have the benefit of knowing that philosophy is the playground of the mind. So I exaggerate my voice when I come to the humorous part of the lecture. I make my body language more than my typical presentation. Sometimes I even say something to the effect of "That was a joke. It's okay to laugh." Often they need permission to relax. So using humor effectively is going to make you pay more attention to how you speak and what you mean. It's going to help you be not only more present when you're talking with others, but it's also going to force you to pay more attention to the audience. When are they lagging? What can I have ready to deal with that lag because it won't always come at seven or eleven minutes into the presentation? Being more aware both of your audience and how you can and do interact with them will make you a better communicator.

There is some benefit to paying attention to comedians and humor writers. If you find them funny, if you appreciate their humor and how they do it, then by all means study them. I am not much for a deadpan sort of delivery style. I like to use comedic gesturing and exaggeration. I want to be both vocally and visually expressive. It's part of the fun of it for me. Whether you're a dead pan sort of person or a more dramatic humorist, just take some time to see how those who do what you do, and study it. You will find that your ability to use humor grows and improves.

The final way in which humor can be helpful in communication is exemplified by this great quote from science fiction writer Isaac Asimov. "Jokes of the proper kind, properly told, can do more to enlighten questions of politics, philosophy, and literature than any number of dull arguments." When you can make a point with a humorous story, or a witty comeback, or use humor to help a message get across, not only will you look better, you'll be more effective. I cannot tell you how many times that a clever little response to a student's question netted me more class comprehension than any of the lecture notes I'd worked so hard to prepare. When I give talks about humor and the workplace, stories that encapsulate what I mean, especially funny ones, have far more effect than simple lecture. Don't get me wrong, my lectures are great (of course they are!), but they're so much better when I can use humor to explain a point. For one particularly difficult topic in the philosophy of science, I rely on a *Spongebob Squarepants* episode, and my students love it. (It's the Sea Bear one: Season 3, Episode 17) They also learn the ideas all the more readily. Definitely a win-win.

Find ways to incorporate humor into your communications. Start small and get a sense for what works under what conditions. What works in an email will not be the same as what works face-to-face, or when you're addressing a large group of folks. But be willing to experiment and play. You'll find both you and your audience more engaged.

Empathy

The humorist and classical pianist Victor Borge once said "laughter is the closest distance between two people." We all know the power of a smile and the warmth of a good laugh. So a good leader knows how to use humor to reach out to people. Good leaders connect with the people they lead. Good leaders don't just seem approachable, they are approachable. This means that the person who shares a laugh with others, who invites others to laugh with them or possibly even at them is going to reach them more effectively.

To know when to use humor, when to rely on a laugh to connect with others, requires a lot. You must know how to "read a room" to see if humor is appropriate. This means that you're paying attention to the body language and all the other non-verbal cues that indicate quite a bit about others. The ability to pay attention to and respond to not only the verbal cues, but non-verbal cues is a cornerstone of empathy. Empathy requires that we imagine what the other feels and then respond to it in an appropriate manner. We can't even begin to know what the other person is feeling unless we're paying attention to them. Basic empathy requires attending to the person.

When I genuinely pay attention to someone, when I imagine what it's like to walk in their shoes, I am practicing empathy. When I choose to use humor to reach out to someone, I am also relying on empathy. When I adjust the humor I use so as to not poke fun at someone, I am using empathy. When I find humor to be the best tool to console someone, I am using empathy. Humor and empathy both have emotional elements that rely on the same skills. A good leader knows that in sharpening the one, one also sharpens the other.

Creativity/Problem Solving

One of the things that attracts me the most about humor is the creativity involved. I have been impressed by kids who've told jokes that are far more creative than I might ever had told. I've been in classrooms where teachers have found some of the most creative ways to explain concepts that made the lesson easier to digest. I routinely steal from them all.

Good jokes, wit, and humor present subtle and not-so-subtle challenges to how we conceptualize the world. They make us recognize relations that we hadn't seen before. My son was doing an online quiz and he was really trying to get first place. He started in third, dropped to 8th, and as he was going he would bounce around. I started messing with him on his performance. He eventually pulled into second place which is pretty good. He was rightfully proud. Being the sort of dad that I am I asked him if he knew what second place meant. I told him that second was just the first loser. He smiled at my tease and then responded that he was going to cry himself to sleep that night. A great comeback for an eleven-year-old who was dealing with the joys of pandemic schooling.

Second place is technically the first loser, but that's not the point. I clearly wasn't making fun of my son. While it's certainly logically correct, the joke is simply meant to poke fun at his success. It's a joke. Being playful with him, messing around with him, shows him that I am paying attention.

I'm not brushing him off. I have to know that he came in second, and I have to know that he is proud of it lest I wouldn't be messing with him. Humor used well allows us to play around and look for the odd connections, explore them, and more importantly enjoy them. Coming in second ain't bad. Part of the humor comes from the inverting of the idea of second place a relating it to being a loser. He got it, and make no mistake, he teases me as well. He most often teases me about my dad-bod. It's an easy go to for him, and it's one that I am a little sensitive about. Hopefully this shows him that I am not so thin-skinned or self-important as to not be able to play with him and him with me. The teases likely wouldn't work if there wasn't some level of reciprocity and more importantly, positive regard.

 Exercise: What are some ways you could be funny as a leader? What about those traits you found that I didn't cover? How does humor as you understand it now, fit in with them? Don't worry if not all of them work out. Humor doesn't need to be everywhere.

CHAPTER 8

Humor Under Pressure

When we normally think of humor we think of comedy, jokes with our friends, all the good times. But humor can also be of great help when times are tough. Whether we're dealing with the throes of a global pandemic, a recent tragedy close to home, or that endless pile of laundry we can never hope to tame, humor not only reminds us that there is something out there beyond the difficulties we face, but that without humor many of those difficulties would be insurmountable.

 Exercise: Can you think of a time when humor helped you deal with an emergency or a tragedy? Describe it. What did the humor do to make you feel better?

Let's get an important fact out of the way. Humor under pressure doesn't just happen. It's not something you're born with, or can just do. Ronald Reagan's famous quip that "He wouldn't use the youth and inexperience of his opponent against him" was not an epiphany he had during the nationally televised debate. He was coached because folks prepping Reagan knew that question was going to surface. They knew he was going to be asked about his age. They also realized that a witty response would, to borrow terms from performers, "kill." And it most certainly did. Because thereafter, his age wasn't an issue. His display of wit, however canned it was, put those worries about age and mental acuity to rest. But if you've been following along and doing some of the exercises in the book, if you've been looking for incongruities and ways to play around with the world around you, you're in a much better position to be funny in times of stress. I still have moments when I come up with a line that I wish I has used at an earlier time, and you will too. Don't see that as a drawback. That means you're still thinking, playing, and creating. Doing that will help you to use humor well under pressure.

 Exercise: What's the funniest pressure or emergency humor bit you've ever heard? No not from a movie!

So why turn to humor under pressure? One of the main reasons that humor under pressure is helpful is that it allows us to be more effective in what we're doing. We can move easier, think quicker and more effectively, and our emotions become not a hindrance but a help. Have you ever been so mad, distraught, or worried, that all you could focus on was solely on the problem which exacerbated your being upset? That's not a good place to be. When you're in a situation where all you can focus on is the negative emotions, you're not going to solve the problem because all you'll see, all you'll feel is the anger or worry. You will not get to dealing with the problem or better still develop a strategy for a solution. Panic and pressure can often create blinders that obscure solutions when we need to solve a problem.

Let me start with two stories of my use of humor in stressful situations. The first is from a time I was traveling home after a conference and going through the security checks at the airport. We all know how unpleasant the airport lines are. We have to take off our shoes, remove belts, empty pockets, disgorge the contents of our last meal—okay not that last one—but the experience isn't fun and it's stressful. People get flustered and tend to muck up easy things like putting back on their belt or shoes. The line grows longer and people feel the impatience and stress grow. I usually mess up my shoes, repacking my bag, much to the chagrin of those around me.

The security line is made all worse when you get through the scan and must then quickly reassemble yourself with the added pressure of not holding up the line. Your belongings are spread over three or four bins. You're trying to consolidate them, get the bins stacked so more people can get through the line. You're trying to get all your things together and maybe the security person asks you "Is this your bag?" Of course the line of bins is now stacking up, no one's happy, everyone's rushed, and you still have to put on your belt, get your shoes, and remember what gate you have to get to because you've forgotten that given the boredom of waiting in line. We should adopt this sort of security for all our gatherings! Imagine the joy of making Nana and Uncle Fred open their bags before coming into your home for the holiday meal!

I have dealt with this situation a number of times. One time it went differently in a very good way. I was traveling home after a conference and was dreading the inevitable security line. I had tried to make my bags and clothing as easy and ready for this process. At least I had my stuff condensed to one bin (thank you restaurant kitchen training). I had made it through the hands-up, tube scan, and was now trying to get my belt on. I was fumbling through what should be a routine process because I was so concerned about all the people behind me. I've put on lots of belt lots of times. I've had to make new holes in my belts (both the good kind and the bad kind). But for some reason this daily task was proving difficult. As I was awkwardly trying to put on my belt I happened to look up and in this airport, there was the sign announcing the "Recombobulation Area." Do an internet image search for "recompbobulation area" and you'll see it. White letters, brown background. The airport paid real money for this sign.

I have to say I laughed a little when I saw it. I paused for sure and smiled, drinking in the humor of that sign. But the best part was after that laugh, I relaxed. That laugh, the little bit of humor made the awkwardness disappear and I put that belt on more quickly and with less stress than I would have. And that included the pause. Instead of doing a bad job of dressing myself, becoming increasingly worried about the folks behind me, and making a simple process awful, and making it take longer, the laugh let me relax. My recombobulation was made all easier for the humor and I didn't miss my flight.

That's the beautiful power of humor in stressful or emergency situations. My ability to relax and do the things I needed to with ease is some of what humor can accomplish in situations where there's a high stress, high pressure feel. It can take much of that stress and pressure and minimize it. And as we saw in chapter 4, there is research that demonstrates the positive effect humor has on making stress seem less so. I encourage you to keep the idea of humor in your back pocket for just such occasions.

The humor in this situation doesn't minimize the stressor or problem. It doesn't even need to make fun of it. The humor has fun with it. That's a crucial difference. Having fun with someone or something is far different than making fun or using the humor to avoid. Even in the most serious of times, I can have fun with someone as we deal with the events. As I am so fond of pointing out, the humor is a great addition, a necessary addition to an environment. Don't overlook humor's importance because we instinctively feel that humor isn't appropriate. It may not be serious, but humor is appropriate and quite useful.

The next story comes from my role as a professor and advisor. Students, especially college students, are highly stressed. They have multiple assignments going, multiple due dates, active lives, and lots of their life isn't within their control. They're often at the whim of inflexible professors like me. As an advisor I help students get through their course choices and other issues necessary for graduation. I had a student, let's call her L.P., who was a new freshman and routinely was in my office with some sort of emergency about school. A class wasn't going well, her roommates were annoying, she'd heard something about classes that wasn't true. L.P. was in a state of near perpetual discombobulation (that's a callback right there). It clearly had a negative effect on her. I must say that I was finding her visits to be tiring too.

One afternoon I was in the main office with a couple of other folks, my boss, our administrative assistant, and a few others when L.P. ran in, face red, breathing hard, exclaiming, "Dr. Mike, Dr. Mike, I need to discuss my future life with you!" Whatever relaxed air had been in the room was gone after she made her exclamation. I thought for a moment and said "Sure. I'd be happy to talk with you about that, but I think I need to discuss some things with my wife first." If you can believe it, her face got redder, but everyone, including her, started laughing. She relaxed, and we went to my office and had a productive discussion.

I've had some people worry that my use of humor with my student in this case was dismissive. Let me assure you it wasn't. My interactions with her as advisor and professor were professional and engaged. I didn't use the humor to dodge an issue, but rather to deflate the upset she felt. I wasn't making fun, I was trying to have a little fun with the process. That's a crucial difference. More importantly, she knew I wasn't dodging her. If I'd have just responded to the "emergency" as an emergency, and jumped right to it, I wouldn't have been able to show her that the issue wasn't that bad. She may have continued panicking and we would have had a less helpful meeting. Certainly if it had been a real emergency, losing our composure wouldn't help with a solution.

I still keep in touch with L.P. and I asked her permission some years ago to relate this story. She jokingly asked which "crisis" it was because she said she had so many. I had already developed and established a relationship of professor and advisor with her. I had come to learn that she tended to exaggerate. I also helped her as any advisor would. She wouldn't have kept coming to me if she had thought I wasn't interested and genuine in my approach. The humor worked for two reasons. We had a relationship, and she trusted me. So the humor that you use in a situation needs to be gauged against a variety of other factors. I wouldn't have started dealing with L.P. with humor in a crisis situation. But once we'd established a good relationship, that she knew I used humor, this was an effective tactic.

There's another lesson here that anyone who wants to use humor can use. Comics often use lighter jokes as they warm up the audience. It helps to build their rapport. Once it's established that the audience is friendly, then they can launch into their more hard-hitting jokes. If you want to use humor, you need to set the ground as one that's receptive to humor use. That prep-work is going to have huge dividends as you use humor more and more.

Exercise: Was there a time when you wished you could have said that funny thing, or came up with one later that would have been perfect? What was it about the situation that made you struggle? How could you make the struggle less so that you might be able to have the funny bit at the ready?

You may be wondering what, if anything, a college philosophy professor can offer about humor and times of stress. What's the most stressful thing about my job? Not getting enough coffee in the morning? Maybe I've not asked "why" enough times today? The two stories above are about stress for sure, but there are no lives hanging in the balance, no existential emergencies needing my attention. True. But they are times of stress, and I've found a good use for humor in dealing with them. But perhaps you're not convinced yet, because these aren't "real" emergencies. Fair enough. Let's look at some other emergency situations where humor was important and helpful.

Here's an example from an actual battlefield. This story was related to me by a British military officer. He and his unit were coming under fire, and one of his soldiers lost a part of an arm in the firefight. Hideous and gruesome for sure. Precisely the sort of time panic seems reasonable. As the officer was trying to get the soldiers organized to regroup and leave, the soldier who had lost his arm was screaming he couldn't leave because "he'd lost his arm." In response another soldier jokingly responded "No you haven't; it's right there," as he gestured to the remains of the arm. As the officer described it, the wounded soldier paused, looked, and then realized the finality of the situation. He broke free of his panic and the troops were able to more successfully deal with the battle.

While I never hope to have to experience something like that, the story points out the power of humor even in the worst of times. There are similar stories of humor on the battlefield. Even the most experienced of soldiers can suffer shock when a firefight begins. There are numerous tales of the nearest other soldier telling the shocked soldier "Hey, isn't there a battle we need to be getting to?" as a way to break through the shock and get the person to engage. The unexpected, out of place and sardonic question has the power to cut through those negative emotions upon which we're transfixed. Just as with the soldier showing the other one where his missing limb was, cut through the panic, well placed humor can help us focus and move on. Humor, even and especially during emergencies, allows us to loosen up and see forest through the trees. In fact, humor is one of the only tools that can do this so easily.

Humor doesn't just have to be used in the emergency. It can be used as a way to deal with a stressful job. The following anecdotes are likely just stories, but they provide a good perspective using humor in the right way. These are morality tales in joke form. As with the above, they come from areas where bodily harm and or death is a definite possibility.

The first comes from someone asking a bomb disposal technician how he handles the stress of the job. It must be enormous. The tech, in response, says something to the effect of "Well I really see there are two outcomes. The first is that I diffuse the bomb and everyone's safe. And that's great. The second is when I don't diffuse the bomb. And, well, it's not my problem anymore." This vignette again shows the power of humor to cut through the clutter and really have us focus on the important facts, the ones that matter. Getting stressed about a bomb going off to the point it negatively influences your ability to do your job helps no one. And yes, let's not sugar coat it, if you screw up, it's likely your last mistake. But look on the bright side, it's your *last* mistake.

There's another great story from the famous Battle of Thermopylae about the soldier and "bravest of all men" Dienekes. He was a Spartan soldier under King Leonidas and this story has been told for millennia and even made it into the movie *300*. Upon being told by an understandably worried soldier that the sheer numbers of arrows that will rain down during the battle from the opposing Persian forces would "block out the sun," Dienekes commented that this was "good news. For now we will fight in the shade."

Dienekes took what was assumed to be a universally bad thing and reframed it to find the brighter side using humor. In so doing, he showed to those around him, the men he led, that humor matters. He modeled a sort of stance that was important to the outlook of his soldiers. He was calm and light, and that carried over into the troops. While the Persian force was strong and vastly outnumbered the Greeks, the Greeks eventually won. I am sure that humor was helpful. It allowed the men around him to face the issues head on without the weight of undue stress.

History has taken these stories, and the use of a wry humor to deal with a difficult topic and created a name that has stuck. Such humor is called laconic, after region where Sparta was located. Another tale, again remembered in history and important enough to be used in the movie *300*, concerns an exchange between King Leonidas and his wife. In response to his wife's question as to what she should do (given that he wasn't likely to come back) as he was leaving for a hopeless battle, Leonidas is said to have responded, "Marry a good man and raise good children." Doesn't get more to the point than that. Why obsess over something that is not going to change? Find a little humor to make it more bearable. The humor you show is a kindness not just to yourself, but to the others you care for as well. Laconic humor, a wry comment here and there not only refocuses us to more productive acts, but also help us do them better, achieve them more readily. Again, humor makes the issues far less stressful.

Our next story is drawn from the medical care arena, and while it uses humor as a technique to cope, it's not particularly funny. Fair warning, it's not going to draw a laugh. It's not supposed to. It exemplifies the use of wit to help deal with a difficult situation. If you're interested in some cases of medical care and humor, check out the book I co-edited with Dr. Stephanie Kelly, *Cases on Applied and Therapeutic Humor*. Yes dear reader that was a shameless self plug.

An infant was born that has a suite of issues and wasn't expected to live long. As is common practice, there was a team of medical professionals all with their specific focus and their approaches on how to treat a particular set of issues. There was really only one prognosis and it was grim. As the team met, they discussed the treatment regimen as if the child was going to live. They took this approach, because that's the approach they typically take. What care do we provide to help the patient recover? Medical care folks generally fight disease to make people better. It's essentially their default setting. An individual among them noticed that the discussion was running on an assumption that the child was going to survive and that the discussed options were neither needed nor appropriate. Instead of trying to point out the flawed assumption and redirect folks in a more "Hey, I think we need to refocus our discussions on the facts of this case" sort of way, a more rational choice perhaps, the individual interrupts and says, "Folks, this kid is more likely to be second base than play second base." Harsh? Yes. Perhaps even brutal. But the point the sardonic statement intends is to refocus the group on the palliative care that needs to be done. Don't waste precious time and energy on a futile pursuit that will end with the same result and possibly make the child's time less pleasant and set people up for failure. Realize the situation for what it is. This statement did more to refocus them, and more to redirect than any more rationally laid out argument could have. And wasting time discussing a treatment pathway that was ultimately going to do no good, was not providing the palliative care that the infant, family, and all those involved knew needed provision.

There are countless stories of individuals using humor in dire situations. From the concentration camps of WWII to journeys of exploration, humor has the ability to lift us up when things are bad. It's no coincidence that levity and lighthearted are how we tend to describe humor. Some prisoners in certain POW camps were tortured with ropes, and when a new prisoner would come in, the "veterans" could be heard to say something to the effect "it's not so bad when you get to know the ropes." The other long-term residents would ruefully smile. I imagine the newbie wouldn't get it at first and then might have laughed a bit later, making the pain of the torture slightly more bearable. You know, "after he'd gotten to know the ropes."

 Exercise: So many of these stories involve reframing the issue so as to highlight something funny, or make something funny. Is there a similarity in how these examples reframed? Do they give you any ideas?

Humor won't heal the cuts, bruises, or scars. But it does make those injuries easier to deal with. Further, when exposed to things like torture and pain, it's not as if one joke, the first joke will bring to the person immediate relief. It takes time. Some say that it takes about twenty jokes to make the humor really work. Now, obviously there hasn't been a lot of research on this topic. I doubt it would ever pass an IRB (institutional review board) at a university, so we're long on theory and short on empirical evidence. But let's be happy with that. If what I've been writing about helps you see the power of humor, then let that be sufficient.

What is happening when we joke about the things that harm us, about the things that cause us pain and stress, is one of the ways that we fight back against this world that can be so cruel. It's the self pushing back, reasserting its role as the one in control. You may be able to hurt me, make me live a certain life, but one of the places all that nastiness can't get to is my ability to use humor and show the world, and more importantly myself, that there are still parts of me, important parts of me that can't be harmed even by the most vicious of circumstance. In so using humor, I rebuild myself. And that's something to be proud of, to smile about, even when it's hard.

 Exercise: How do you feel now about humor in tragic, stressful, or difficult situations? Has what you read encouraged you to try to use more humor in situations such as these? If yes, how will you make yourself better able to use humor?

CHAPTER 9

Office Humor

One of the things I hear a lot as I give talks and work with people on bringing more humor into their lives, is that everyone is so uptight. *We can't joke about anything anymore. TV shows that were made only a few years ago would never be allowed to air now. I am so worried about offending someone, so many people are too thin-skinned and can't take a joke.* Nowhere is this hesitance or fear of using humor felt more than in the workplace. It's one of the reasons people have such a negative and fearful attitude to using humor in all but the most personal of spaces.

 Exercise: Does your organization and or the people you work with use much humor? Does it tend to be of a certain type? Do/Can you make fun, make witty observations?

To fix all the problems mentioned above would be the work of a lifetime. We've had years to get us to this position. It will take time to get a more meaningful presence of humor in our lives. But it's a journey worth starting. I am not going to take too many sides on issues of political correctness, or being too uptight, etc. The above shouldn't be taken as me endorsing those worries. I'm not. The world is a diverse place, and as humor practitioners we need to be aware of this. One person's reason to laugh might be another's reason to cry. Humor can be a wonderful way to create and strengthen relationships, and it can also be the source of isolation. I have been the object of ridicule, and it's rarely fun. I've also ridiculed others—not some of my better moments. Ridicule is best avoided. Don't make fun, just as your mom told you.

The important thing to remember when trying to find and use humor in your organization is to focus on some of things we've already covered. There are lots of ways to use humor effectively that don't require ridicule. Focus on the idea of incongruity, and remember that the work world is full of them. You know it. You see them every day. There's more than enough there for a lifetime of laughs. One of the areas of where you can begin to find lurking incongruities is in the everyday things you and your co-workers do. At the time of writing this I am teaching from home because of the COVID-19 pandemic. I have been absent from my office nearly eighteen months now. The fact that my life and the lives of many of us are relegated to screens is a crazy development. It's where we are and likely where we'll be for the future as well. But there's a lot of funny in those screens. Dig in.

While adjusting to teaching online and moving all interactions to a digital format was a bit of a shock, I've noticed a few odd things. One of the odd behaviors to do with meetings. For some reason, at the close of most online meetings people raise their voices to say goodbye and then wave. Think about that. We're waving goodbye to people on a digital meeting. We don't wave goodbye when we leave our face-to-face meetings. I don't wave goodbye to my students when I leave a class. Why are we compelled to do so in meetings? Imagine at the end of a regular face-to-face meeting you raised your voice and exclaimed, "Everyone take care." Could you imagine waving goodbye to your boss as you left the weekly meeting? I rarely say goodbye after a face-to-face meeting. In fact, I am not sure I ever have. We don't use that sort of closing behavior in in-person meetings.

It's a strange set of behaviors. It's like we ported over this behavior from a phone call, which makes sense. On the phone, when we can't see anyone, the goodbye lets us know that the hanging up is about to happen. In a face-to-face meeting we need no such signals. Everyone just gets up. Of course on Zoom meetings now, getting up is discouraged as we've all adopted the business up top and sweat pants, shorts, or no pants on the bottom approach. But more importantly, the way we end the online meeting is just clicking an end meeting button. There's an awkward lull as the less dexterous computer users float the cursor over the button and everyone's face is in a search mode while we all blink out of our virtual existence one by one. There's a comedy special there to be sure.

Exercise: Have you noticed anything weird about our digital meeting behaviors?

This whole online and remote situation is a great ground for incongruities. Not only are you poking fun at something we all do and thus can all relate to, you're using a little self-deprecating humor, which is often helpful. The best way to start joking about these oddities would be to ask the rhetorical question, "Ever wondered why we wave goodbye at the end of online meetings? I find it so odd. I do it and I have no idea why!" This is great for a couple reasons. First, you begin with your observations and tie the incongruities to yourself. Second, you invite a coworker or friend to see the world as you do. Third, you ask them to do the "yes and" response. When you invite them in and ask for their input, you're not only engaging them, you're engaging them in a way that promotes a humorous response. If the conversation takes, you'll soon be sharing all sorts of oddities. You'll get to know those around you in a different way, and they'll get to know you. You will also open up the space for people to let off a little steam through good-natured gripes. The initial humorous observation lays the groundwork to make all this happen because in many ways, laughter is like meetings. If you have one, it's easier to have a second.

Another way to think about humor in the workplace is to remember the house allegory from Chapter 2. Those incongruities about the meetings are things that anyone who's had to shift to a digital format has likely experienced. It's low-level; you're poking fun at a shared experience. You're not saying it's wrong, you're simply noting the strangeness of the practice. I mean, what else is there to do? If at the close of a meeting, you just dropped out without some sort of signal, it might lead people to think you'd been inappropriately dropped due to a technological error. They may hang out or try to reach you from another messaging app or alternative digital communication platform. By focusing on incongruities and poking at a shared experience centered on digital meetings, you get to play around with others and show that levity is an accepted, valued, and used thing. There's a technique improv folks use to help increase play mentioned above, so we'll discuss it now below.

*Exercise: Imagine if you could just put up
an icon, or maybe an image with only your
name in a face-to-face meeting? That would
be hilarious. Maybe you should give everyone
an icon for an in-person meeting just for
laughs. There's a practical joke in their as
we move back into a post-pandemic life.*

Improvisational comedy, or improv, turns out to be a wonderfully rich area
to mine if you want to get some help in bringing humor into your organization. "Yes and. . ." is a classic exercise that comedians and performers use to
tap into spontaneity and creativity. The idea is to have someone begin an
improv session with an idea and then the next person takes the idea and extend it by thinking "*yes, and. . .*" They extend the idea in a way that respects
the original idea, and then adds their unique input. This technique works
because it asks you to focus not on what you think about the idea, but how
you can enhance it. How can you work with it and grow it? It's collaborative.
It focuses on creating commonalities. It's both challenging and lots of fun.

I use the "yes, and. . ." approach as a ground rule in my classes when
we discuss topics. One of things students love to do is critique and explain
how another's view is wrong. Starting a conversation with essentially a 'no'
response is surefire way to shut it down before it gets started. I mean, it is a
philosophy class after all. While critique is a helpful skill at times and often
necessary as we refine our ideas, it's often the case that students won't fully
appreciate a view and provide a critique that's unfair. Furthermore, it's not
like the first pass at anything is going to give us the end product. All ideas
take time, attention, and refinement. Part of coming up with a good idea is
the development part. Instant critique can shut ideas down that could do
well with a little development. I tell students to spend at least five or so minutes promoting the view. Assume "yes, it's right" and then think how you
can add to it. What else supports this proposed view? Practice, "Yes, and. . ."

I do this for a couple of reasons. The first is that it makes our discussions richer. If I offer an idea, and you immediately point out a flaw, there's
no further chance for growth. It limits possibilities, and that's harmful if we
want to develop resilience, perseverance and what we now call a growth
mindset. The second reason is that it forces the students to respond in a way
that makes them think harder. To faithfully complete the "yes and" thought
means that you have to understand what's going on with the original prompt.
Many students, and adults, have difficulty overcoming their own views and
biases. If we want to encourage growth, critique has its place. But initially,

let the idea go. Give it space to grow. The third reason I use it is because it's fun. I get to remind students, "hey we're playing the build it up game, not the tear it down." Construction may be harder, but it also a lot more rewarding. The students get to play around with an idea that isn't theirs, and develop it. This is one of the more powerful learning experiences.

Focusing on "yes, and. . ." relates to our organizations in many ways because we're tapping into that same desire to play, to look at the world that energizes my students. If you approach more of your organizational interactions with this happy, constructive attitude, people will enjoy times in meetings more. They'll find the organizational space one they enjoy being a part of. Bring people in to discuss growth and in so doing you're allowing them to practice growth. Invite them to the "yes, and. . ." party. When we all share something like the "yes, and. . ." experience it's an important early step to creating an organizational space to where levity and laughter will blossom. Further, it strengthens to cohesion of the work group. Together they accomplish something valuable. Instead of simply reporting in, checking in, or checking up, the meeting becomes a more dynamic space.

If you're not ready to drop right into improv techniques, or going straight for jokes and comedy, then start easier with play. One of the bases for creating an environment that's amenable to humor is to encourage play. I am not talking about kickball in the corridor, or hide and seek among the cubicles, though a fun treasure hunt may be appropriate, but rather play in the ways that you communicate.

Emails are a great place to encourage play. Some companies end mass emails with a pun. Lots of drink companies put playful messages on the underside of their caps. For a while, my friends and I used to compare them at lunch. Now puns may not be your thing, and maybe you don't have bottle caps available, but don't despair. Look for similar ways you can drop humor into your work. Remember, the moment people start looking for the playful elements of the email they're now interacting with the message in a totally new way. Just like those Oxo handles on the vegetable peeler, they will enjoy it. Lots of companies will "play" with their customers in easy places like labels, instructions, or even barcodes. Do an internet search under "funny barcodes." You'll be glad you did.

Once people engage in play in something like an email, they're no longer simply "looking at the words," pretending to read. They have begun to actually read and look for content. They're paying attention in an entirely new and more engaging fashion. If the bit of information is buried in a riddle, they have to read carefully and think. Most importantly, they are not in that disengaged readership that so many of us fall into when we get mass emails. They're looking around. So figure out ways to bury Easter eggs in your emails. If you're the author of your mass emails, then be an author. Don't simply aggregate data and send it out. When readers feel that this is all stuff they can get off the web, they won't read—they'll just wait to search it on the website or ask Harry down the hall.

There are other ways to encourage play. We all have difficult things we have to deal with in our job. If there's something that you and your coworkers face on a regular basis that's a perfect place to begin. I was speaking to an Army Recruiter and she was lamenting how it was hard on new members of the staff to deal with the high levels of rejection they get. The Armed Forces of the United States, while a noble calling, is a hard sell—especially to young people. These new recruiters are chosen because they have been successful in other places. Then they get to the new duty posting and they don't nearly as well or achieve the levels of success they had earlier. It's understandably hard.

When I heard her issues, I suggested that they have a little playful competition. Each person posts on a note in the main area detailing the best rejection, or best tale of woe during a certain period of time: a week or a month, whatever time works best for your job. Don't run from the failure. Run at it, playing with it. Poking fun at it makes the difficulties seem less so. Ridicule it, this is a perfect time for some clap backs. Once there are enough or the time limit has expired, the group gets together. The folks vote on the worst/best rejection and then the winner, or loser, gets a (consolation) prize. This is sure to boost morale and it will help people see the sorts of things they'll deal with and develop strategies to deal with them. It will also show that everyone experiences these sorts of things. Running at the failures with your friends and colleagues smiling and laughing there with you makes it all the easier. Who knows, you all may find new and creative ways to deal with those failures. In fact, I'm sure you will.

If you're unsure which sorts of failures and challenges are appropriate to bond over, I have a solution. If you want to know the sorts of things that really bother us, look at the things people gripe about. Gripes tell us a lot about our workspaces and the challenges we face.

Griping isn't complaining. We gripe about different things than we complain about. I complain to my boss on something that I think should be corrected. Complaints are formal, and need addressing in a way that effects change. In contrast, I gripe about the stuff that I don't think will change. I gripe about the weather. I gripe about traffic. I even gripe about the dog hair all over the house because of our two dogs. We gripe about things beyond our control.

One of the best gripes I ever heard came from a student when he came into class. It was rainy and cold, and overall unpleasant. It had been that way for a while. The students and I were griping about the weather and this student chimed in, "The weather is just disrespectful." I actually laughed out loud at it. It was such a poetically grumpy way to describe the weather. More importantly I kept it and use it sometimes. It rarely fails to get a laugh. Don't think you have to come up with the new and funny things all the time. That you can beg, borrow, and steal from other funny people is yet another reason to love humor. In fact, comedian Mike Stankiewicz once said, "I built my act by hanging out with funnier people."

When it comes to humor in the office, teasing has to come up. And before you get ready for the "don't tease" lecture, that's not what I am going to do. Teasing isn't all bad. In fact in can be quite helpful. I tease my wife and she me, and we're still married. Some have argued that it's because we tease each other that we're still married. I tease my kids, and they haven't been to therapy yet—but I'm working on it. They now tease me. I even tease students sometimes. My little joke to my student L.P. back in chapter 8 was a sort of tease. Teasing isn't all bad, but as with humor, the how is important.

Office teasing has been around ever since there were offices and likely way before. When we normally think of teasing the concept is typically seen as a negative sort of behavior. But there's a lot of research to suggest that teasing isn't as bad as we think. In fact, in groups where teasing is present, that group is likely pretty well bonded. Groups where teasing is largely absent might not even be real groups after all. If you think about it, you don't tease people you don't know. You tease people you do. And often it's done in friendly way. If I don't tease you it probably means that we're not all that close.

Don't get me wrong, teasing can be mean-spirited, intend to do harm, and accomplish that. This sort of teasing is called bullying. If you find yourself teasing someone, and somewhere, no matter how deep down, you're using that tease as a proxy for anger, or to hurt, or annoy, you're probably better served to not tease in those conditions. It'd be best to try and figure out why you're teasing that person in that way.

But we can also use teasing in what's called a prosocial way. As a way to playfully make a point, there isn't a clean and clear line to draw here. Teasing requires at least two people and no matter how close you are to the person, sometimes the friendliest of teases may hurt. Think of both your intent in teasing and its effect. They aren't always going to correspond. I've had bad days when people teasing me just didn't go over well and others where a tease provided a much needed kick in my backside.

One story that I love to relate when it comes to teasing happened early on at a university I work for. I am a white guy, and I had been hired as the honors director at an HBCU (historically black college or university). My assistant director at the time was an older black lady who helped me in ways

I am probably only now realizing and likely never will fully appreciate. I had been working in my new job for about five months, and our new office space had me sharing a wall with her. I was not doing too well at some computer work and I knocked on the wall and asked her to come over and help me. She knew the system way better than I did, and she had been helping me. I clearly wasn't a good student of her lessons. As I turned to face her as she walked into the room, she quipped "Yes Masser?" Apparently my face turned bright red (hard to hide when you're white) and she immediately stifled a laugh and said, "I'm sorry."

I had a decision to make. She was obviously just trying to mess with me. But the content of that tease could get me fired and off campus without a chance to even gather my books. I could have tried to ignore it, and just gone to the problem at hand, but my embarrassment and discomfort were written all over my face. To try and just ignore it would have told her I wasn't comfortable with even discussing the topic: that she'd crossed a line. It would have created a distance between us. A distance I wouldn't want. I could have responded by making a formal, boss-type of statement saying, "I understand what you're trying to do and while I get it. Please understand it's not appropriate for a work environment. I could lose my job. Blah, blah." This sort of administrative doublespeak is a dodge. However appropriate that response might have been, it would have created more distance between us. Again, this was not what I wanted.

I chose to accept the tease for what it was—a joke. She was messing with me and, her taking that step to mess with me indicated that she saw us as being coworkers who were close enough that we could joke and tease. This is an important milestone. Of course she, being a black woman, gets to make jokes of those sorts, whereas I don't. So what I said, after I hope my face was less red, "That was a good one. No need to apologize. I get it. And as someone who loves humor and messing with someone, you got me. You got me good. You got me so good! But you do realize that if anyone ever hears you talk to me like that in this office, I won't make it to the car. I doubt I'd even get my last paycheck." She got it, and the best part was that my response brought us closer together. I *was* someone she could mess with. I thought and still think it was a great joke/tease. I have a much richer life for the experience. Plus that story usually gets lots of laughs.

Teasing is not always easy and is made more difficult by the various ways in which our backgrounds and experiences are different. Teasing is not something you begin with in general. It's something that builds up and develops over time. You wouldn't tease someone if you were just at the front door (thank you humor as a house allegory from chapter 2—Is one allowed to do a shameless self-plug/callback in their own book?) There needs to be a sense that one knows the person, one knows them to be someone who is merely teasing and not bullying. We only develop these judgments over time. But if you have group of folks in an organization that have been together for a while and teasing is absent, then you've likely got a group that's not an engaged with one another as they could be. Andrew Carnegie was right when he said, "Where there's little laughter, there's little success."

Prosocial teasing is all about the relationships they occur within. One of the ways we know when a tease is playful and friendly depends a lot on how well we know the person. The same tease made to a stranger as opposed to made to a friend will garner different responses. If my friends think I am generally a good fellow, that I tease in playful ways, then they're likely to take my teases in the spirit they were offered. A stranger has no such background to rely upon. So there's a rule. Teasing will work best in situations where the actors know one another. Don't tease strangers. Teasing is to be done in groups where there is already a wealth of fellowship and good faith. When there's a solid relationship, the teasing can be quite a great way to bond, and it can deal with some rather difficult topics as my example above.

We spend a lot of our lives in various organizational spaces. The office, the social group, our faith groups, reading groups, etc. Good working organizations, ones that are engaged, have engaged members, and grow and are effective have humor as a part of their culture. Often that humor will take the form of gentle and playful teases. If your organizational culture lacks humor, there are other problems probably too. Creating humor is easy and low risk, but you do have to work at it. My suggestion is that you start slow and be ready for some failures. They won't be spectacular failures, but failure is tough. Don't get discouraged. Open yourself up to new forms of humor. You'll find that if you do, the organizational spaces will open up as well.

CHAPTER 10

Classrooms and Teaching Spaces

We will all find ourselves teaching something to someone at some point. Whether we're teaching our children, doing on-the-job training, or like me, educating students on the wonderful world of philosophy. Teaching is universal. More importantly, we wouldn't be where we are as a civilization if we didn't teach one another. Teaching is one of the basic gifts we give to each other. I love to learn, meet new people, and find out new ways to do stuff. Just as humor brings us delight because of the incongruities that abound in the world, enjoying learning exercises the same parts of our brains and taps into the same reward system in learning.

The one thing about teaching that no one can get past, that no trick will ever hide, is that learning is work. It can be fun work or it can be drudgery. It can be easy or it can be hard. But no matter what, learning is a process that requires us to be present. Whether you're a teacher like me or an occasional bearer of wisdom, you will have to teach. The most effective teachers often use humor.

You may be thinking that you can skip this chapter if you're not a teacher, and by all means, skip around. This book isn't meant to be a forced march. But even if teaching isn't one of your main pursuits or a side gig, there are some tips and tricks in here, some facts about humor and humor comprehension, about how you can use it to encourage engagement and learning that will be helpful for anyone whether they're a full-time educator or not. Plus there are some funny stories too.

MIRTH

Exercise: Have you had any funny teachers? What do you remember of them?

The main goal of teaching, as if I need to say it, is to impart knowledge or skill. Whether you're teaching someone to do a thing like ride a bike, factor an equation, a new dance step, telling them about some historical event, or even (wait for it) a philosophical concept, humor is a great companion in that quest. As with any tool you need to know how and when to use it. As enjoyable as we would all like the classroom experience to be, learning things can be and sometimes is difficult. No amount of laughter can change that. There have been times where we all struggled with some new process or understanding some new idea. Short selling in the stock market is a concept that makes my brain hurt. Whether I struggled or it came easy, I do know that when I found humor in learning, it made the learning all the easier. Here's a couple examples.

When I was in graduate school I didn't have a lot of confidence. Academia is filled with a lot, I mean a lot a lot, of rejection. So is book publishing too as I have learned. Couple that with the fact that getting a job in philosophy was not a prospect filled with hope, and let's just say that many of us grad students went to the bar more than we should have. I was lamenting all this with my advisor, John Bickle, and he just said. "It's philosophy Mike. Everybody's wrong." That sardonic statement made me smile. It reframed what I was doing. Right or wrong wasn't the end goal, it was the way we worked toward those intellectual goals, knowing full well we'd likely never get *the* right answer. This is not an original sentiment. Lots of experts are very aware of the limits of their knowledge (it's why academics make for boring interviews), but grad students often labor under the idea that they're revealing the truth. That's false. The truth is, on our best days, we're trying to remove error. If truth comes out in the wash, that's a bonus.

The next example I have comes from the concept of perfect. I do philosophy (yes I do have to keep saying that), and for most of my students the concept of the Christian Heaven comes up. One of the ways to describe Heaven is to say it's perfect. Often they think that perfect means, among other things, unchanging. I then look at them and say something to the effect of "Huh, I guess Heaven's boring then. I mean if it never changes wouldn't that just be boring for all of eternity?" Truth is, this little joke is how I came to understand an issue with perfection and heaven. I had that thought. A better person might have taken that insight and gone on to a career in comedy. I went to grad school and look how that turned out.

The first hurdle one faces in any classroom is capturing people's attention. If you can succeed at that, you've done a lot of the heavy lifting when it comes to teaching. Humor, as I've noted in other chapters, is great at capturing attention. The very nature of the humorous incongruity is attention grabbing. Use that to help keep people's attention focused. While we all can and do lose focus as we learn, if you catch something that doesn't fit, that's incongruous, it means that you were in some important respects, paying attention. That's a big part.

Whether you're walking into a teaching space for the first time or for the hundredth time, finding a way to throw some humor in up front is helpful. As the teacher, people already see you as the expert. You are stepping into the space with a sense of authority. This same idea can be applied to leaders as well. How you use that authority is going to influence how receptive folks are to you. Some teachers I know consciously violate the expectation of the staid professor by wearing funny ties, or dressing down, to reduce the sense of hierarchy. I've worn a Spongebob Squarepants shirt to teach in. This really gets students thinking about me. I was once known on my campus as the "guy that wore the Spongebob shirt in class." When you violate expectations, when those violations are viewed as playful or non-serious, you've done two things. You've created and fostered interest, and you've removed some of the hierarchical feel that is sometimes less helpful for an open learning environment.

These harmless violations in dress or manner are particularly helpful for people who are teaching in a short-term space. Think of corporate trainers. They come in for an hour or two, maybe as long as a week, but the end point of the class is in the near term. They need to be able to establish relationships with folks in short order. If they come in with something unique in their dress, it sends a signal. A signal that people pick up on. Not only that, it causes the audience to immediately pay more attention. Wear boring attire and you'll start off with people tuning you out. Having a nice shirt color, or scarf, or cummerbund (I've always wanted to type that word), draws the audience in and helps generate a good rapport. Try out a memorable tie. Add some flair. Perhaps you've just been invited to talk to a group interested in something you're an expert on, and it's a one-off sort of event. Having a way to break the ice through a carefully selected violation is a good start. Maybe you can playfully forego titles. I do.

In my classes I tend to go by Dr. Mike. Dr. Cundall is fine as some students, and even colleagues value that level of formality. But I like to be called Dr Mike. I will often tell colleagues, or other folks that the Dr. is used only in class, formal emails, or when I am making a point about my pedigree—a point that most people needn't concern themselves with to be honest. Most of the time, those letters don't mean all that much. They certainly mean less than folks assume. This playful banter is often enough to set folks at ease and it tells them about me. I am not some nameless knowledge conduit. I'm Dr. Mike, and I am friendly and not too caught up in formality. But the Dr. is important because it also tells the student that I have certain credentials and I am an expert in the field. The banter I use in class isn't exactly humor, but it's close to humor: it's playfulness. Playfulness, as we know, is a necessary ground for humor.

Exercise: What sorts of tricks and funny bits from classes do you recall other teachers using? Have you ever thought, "That was cool" and wanted to emulate it? If so, write them down, remember them, adapt them to your teaching style (yes you have a style). Don't be afraid to imitate—it's flattering remember?

Another general comment about humor and attention. Studies have shown that we all have natural cycles of attention. Every seven to ten minutes even the most disciplined of us will lose focus and our minds will drift. In writing these chapters I've had to stand up, re-focus, a number of times. Don't fight that. Don't expect everyone to have a continuous laser focus in the classroom setting. Since you know this, plan for those breaks or lulls. Incorporate ways to regain attention by adding in incongruities into your presentation, teaching style, lecture, or whatever your preferred mode is. People will not only regain focus, they will be on the look-out for subsequent ones. This means they're paying more attention than at first. This is an easy little hack you can start working on as soon as you go to your next meeting or have to give a presentation.

Students in college tend to give professors a lot of credit—some deserved and some not. As a result, I've often thought about doing a class lecture on a topic and simply lie about the content to just see if the students catch onto it. But I've always thought that might be a bit too much. That violation would hardly be benign, even if I am making a point about paying attention. Figure that over the course of an hour you'll need four to six "breaks" to refocus attention. They don't all have to be humor breaks, but they need to be breaks of a sort. One of my favorites in class is to refer to something from earlier in the class, usually a few weeks prior, and then when the students look confused, quip "Yeah, you didn't think we'd be building on those other concepts, but here we are doing it anyway."

For those of us who are teaching as a more regular part of our daily activities, that is we teach over a long term, the use of humor needs to be a little different. One mistake people make with humor and using it, is that they will take it too far. Humor overdone, overused, is not going to help you reach the goals you've set for yourself as a teacher or for the learner. Humor works best when it accentuates and highlights what you're doing in ways related to the topics at hand. If you're constantly using jokes and humor, if they take up more of your class time than content, then you're doing too much. Even comedians need to break from the jokes to provide a set up so that the joke can work. You need the serious, the direct, so the humor can have a background to stand out from. You're not a comedian, so don't turn your teaching space into a comedy club.

 Exercise: What benign violation or playful element could you add to your class presentation that might foster humor or playfulness?

In a situation where you're routinely meeting with the same class, it's good to set a pattern. Maybe you begin the class with a funny or interesting story. Warm up the class and don't just get right to the new material—this is pretty much the same advice I gave earlier about meetings. Can you find a way to reframe a difficult topic that you've recently covered? When I talk about the concept of argument, one of my go to's to get folks chatting is to bring up the GOAT (greatest of all time) in professional basketball. There are no end of opinions and the vehemence with which people hold their views on the GOAT topic. We go through all the metrics, the titles, the MVP's etc. Usually folks get the idea that it's a tough debate and are more aware of strengths of opposing opinions, while some doggedly stick to their guns. But at the end of all of it I ask a sarcastic question. "Does settling this debate really even matter?! I mean, does answering this question help our society progress?"

These questions reframe the issue because it unexpectedly highlights an assumption some of us had been working under. That the GOAT is an issue worthy of debate. I'll offer my view that Jordan and LeBron (the two main contenders) are luminaries—they're superlative and generational talents. Enough said. Instead of being something we should doggedly or dogmatically worry over, perhaps we shouldn't. I don't see any grand social issues being solved if someone happens to settle this question. Discussing this topic does help us to understand better the idea of argument, but it's not as if any real prize is won if some answer was given and thereby accepted. So relax, have fun with the argument, but don't get all wrapped up in a debate that's not going to accomplish much.

Exercise: Take a moment to watch teachers, corporate trainers, TED Talk speakers, and presenters, etc. and focus on how they manage keeping folks' attention. You're looking at how they practice the craft, not what they're teaching.

One of the final things I want to cover about humor and teaching comes from the creativity of humor and how it makes us think more and harder—sometimes quite a bit harder—about a topic. Let's begin with a little joke I heard from a colleague, Steve Gimbel, who is a far better joke teller than I. It's likely he's funnier too. He is a comedian and a philosopher after all.

> "Abraham and Rebecca opened a little restaurant. On the first day they opened, their first customer was none other than the rabbi. Nervously, Abraham greeted him and handed him a menu. Looking it over, the rabbi ordered roast beef. Abraham thanked him and went back to the kitchen. He told Sarah that this was not only their first customer, but the rabbi, so it had to be good. He took out the order and the two watched anxiously through the little windows in the door. When the rabbi finished, Abraham cleared his plate and asked how he enjoyed the meal. The rabbi responded, 'It was wonderful. There's only one thing. It's so small. I don't even want to say it.' 'Please, rabbi,' responded Abraham, 'if we are to improve, we must know.' 'Well,' said the rabbi, 'it could use more bread. Two slices, maybe it isn't enough.' The next week the rabbi came in and ordered roast beef again. This time they gave him four slices. Afterward, again, he told Abraham that it was delicious but could use more bread. Next week six slices. Still 'could use more bread.' The following week eight slices. Still, 'could use more bread.' The next week, when the rabbi came in, Abraham took an entire loaf of rye bread, cut it in half and put it on the table. After the meal, Abraham went to the table and asked the rabbi how his meal was. The rabbi said, 'Delicious as always, but tell me, why did you go back to just two slices?'"

I had never heard this joke before. He related it as a part of a reminiscence about his grandfather, from whom he'd heard the joke. He recalled that the joke wasn't terribly funny. It was a more a light-hearted morality tale. The moral my colleague takes from this tale/joke is that "some people are never satisfied." This is clearly evidenced by the behavior of the rabbi. One could also offer another interpretation that the rabbi was making a point, that the attempt to please every customer is a fool's game. Take which ever you like.

But if you like my take, let me know. I've a fiver riding on my interpretation being the best. My colleague needs to pay up.

Aside from the implied morality tale of the joke, Steve relates the story because his grandfather told it as a sort of tease. Apparently when his grandfather, a notorious jokester himself, told jokes, they were typically told not for amusement, but to get people to think about things differently. He would often respond to the surprise or confusion of the listener with "You didn't think of it like that did you?" The point of the joke was not amusement, though if it produced a chuckle or a laugh that was an added benefit. The anecdote was offered to challenge your thinking. Jokes can challenge us. When we resolve the confusion or make sense of the incongruity, we are learning something new. Given the obvious power of humor to promote careful thinking, then we clearly need to be using a lot more humor in our teaching.

So why am I talking about my colleague and his grandfather? Surely sitting at your grandfather's side listening to a joke here and there is far different than a classroom. I am offering this so that you realize that while the KISS (keep it simple silly) rule is a good rule in a lot of ways, sometimes we need to be challenged and pushed and forced to more heavy lifting in order to learn and grow. You can use jokes not only to challenge folks, but to encourage attention, and have them learn more deeply and more rapidly. Let me use a couple examples from my own teaching to make the point.

To remind you about my recent history as a teacher, I teach at an historically black college or university NCA&T State University in North Carolina. I also happen to be a white guy. Most of my students are black or African-American, as are most of my colleagues. I was also the director of the honors program. It's why I was brought to the university. The issue of me being white will come up on occasion, especially in class. It's written, as it were, all over my face. Some students are up-front about it and are very direct and others are more circumspect. Regardless of whether the issue comes up on the first day of class or sometime later, it will come up.

I tend not to approach the issue like "Right, so I am white. Let's discuss." This is a little blunt and can be off-putting for some. The issue itself is also difficult given the traditional mission of HBCU's and the state of race relations in the USA. Instead of using the more direct language, I take a more indirect, humor-based tactic. I will often find a way to address my whiteness by saying "As you may have noted, you see that I am a bit melanin-challenged. Let's talk about that." It may take a moment for folks to get the joke, but usually they do, and the pleasant humor makes the upcoming discussion, which can be fraught with the possibility of offense, easier to begin. But the "melanin-challenged" bit (which I am proud of by the way) makes them stop and think about what I just said. They have to expend more cognitive resources to put together that "melanin-challenged" is my way of saying "I'm white." Of course, none of this needs to be said, because I am pretty white, blue-eyes, lighter colored hair and all. The point is that this way of talking isn't simple, it's cognitively demanding. It makes them work to get it. Not only do they enjoy solving the problem, they enjoy the humor that the whole spiel or bit uses. I use the word 'bit' quite consciously. Teaching has a good deal of performance elements to it. Comedians use bits in their acts. You should too when appropriate.

 Exercise: Write some jokes about some difficult topics in your field. They won't all be winners, they'll likely be more losers, but there will be some gems. You'll have to test them out to separate the two.

There's another place where I use the same approach. As the director of the honors program, I am used to dealing with students who are obsessed with grades. Most students are good folks. They want to do well and learn. But honors students tend to be high-drive, high-achieving, and high-mainte-nance. When you burn the candle at both ends, stress is a huge issue. Also, many of these students are used to doing well without always having to work hard. College can often be a shock. Usually around the time of midterms or the beginning of the next semester, I will have some students come to me with grade worries. They are not staring at a row of A's. Sometimes the letters are perhaps more rounded. See what I did there? They're not used to that. So they get worried. They stress a lot. This is understandable given the high value attached to grades and doing well.

To get them to think about how to deal with the situation and create helpful strategies, I will often tell them first that we need to calm down. Of course when has telling someone to "calm down" ever really worked? It's like when people hear I study humor and then ask me to be funny right there. Once I even had a president of a university I was interviewing at, who had read my CV, ask me to tell a joke at the end of our interview. I've never been more nervous because a bad joke could have tanked that interview right there. The joke I chose worked out well as I got some good laughs, but had it flopped, I might not be writing this book now. But back to helping students with anxiety, to put the students at ease, I will invite them, if they're interested, to look at my undergraduate transcripts. I advise them that in my first two years there aren't a lot of vowels to be found. It takes them a second, but they get it. When they do, I then clarify and say "yeah, I wasn't the best student early on, but I managed to figure it out."

The humor here has the same benefits as the above. The roundabout way of describing my less than stellar early years in undergrad makes them forget their plight for a moment. It's a needed distraction. Their focus on figuring out the statement makes them rely on the "figure it out" part of their brain rather than the "panic" part. Once they get the joke, they feel a little better too. I also use the roundabout ways of mentioning non-A grades to good effect. I remove some of the negativity surrounding all those less than angular grades (though the worst grade is chock full of 90 degree angles. . .and now it's a running gag). These little jokes make the later difficult discussion much easier to begin and make progress on. Sometimes the outcome is not what anyone would have wanted, but at least we can deal with it. They know what they need to do. Sometimes they realize that the problems are solvable and work with me to craft appropriate solutions. But that humor, that distraction, that levity all helped create the proper ground so as to move forward in a productive way.

My use of a more "complicated" way of talking about things shows that humor doesn't always simplify. If incongruity is key, then that recognition and subsequent sense making of the issue is actually not simple, it's a long walk cognitively speaking. They have to do more work. This shows us that humor can make us work harder and we enjoy it more. Imagine the power there. You're tricking your class into doing more and they're enjoying it. If I could do that routinely, I would be the best teacher ever. We might even have hordes of philosophers walking the streets. Imagine all the togas, all the 'Why?' questions! It would be a paradise.

Regardless of whether your organizational environment is a classroom, a factory floor, a boardroom, or a kitchen in a restaurant, using humor in these subtle and context shaping ways is crucial to creating a successful culture. Organizational culture is a huge issue. We're often asked to look at ways to change a culture or make these grand changes. This leads us to think in ways that are grand and sweeping. We try to move mountains. Rome wasn't built in a day. The best laid plans of mice and men. . . well you get the point. Perhaps instead of focusing on only the heavy lifting, we can focus on these littler, but no less important things like humor, levity, and enjoyment. They make the later heavy lifting all the easier. As any comic will tell you, getting the first laugh makes getting the second one easier. When we're enjoying things, when the organizational mood is lighter, the mountains we need to move become molehills thereby making the change in a culture become all the easier to achieve. This is the power of humor.

CHAPTER 11

Electronic Laughs and Digital Spaces

We live in a digital world: the world of Zoom meetings (thanks COVID-19), of Google Groups, and Microsoft Teams, of reddit and the infinite universe of sub-reddits, and last but not least memes, YouTube, and Instagram. Some of us are digital natives, others comfortable immigrants, while others struggle to feel at home. Like it or not, the digital world of 0's and 1's, of tweets, and viral sensations, is the world we have. Humor is as much a part of that world as any other, perhaps even more so given the large number of animal fail videos and memes out there. Like humor in meetings, or humor with strangers, there are some decent rules of thumb that will help you out in getting better at using humor in the digital space. The same basic tricks I've been discussing in the previous chapters apply in our online environment. But since we don't have all the same cues and behaviors as we do when we're in a face-to-face setting, there are some things you can do to make sure that your humor is more effective.

 Exercise: What are some of your go-to funny videos, memes, or other web-based content? Is there anything similar about them? (Trust me, Google already knows if there is)

The first rule we need to cover in helping us to better understand and use humor in the digital world is a rule born of the early Internet—when it was more text based and less populated with images. It's called Poe's Law. Poe's

Law states, that in any attempt at satire, humor, of laughter on the internet, one must be careful and clearly mark their communications as humorous. In the early stages of the Internet, long before emoji's became a thing, the ;-) arrangement of punctuation marks was deemed sufficient to indicate that you were trying to be funny. That was the solution to the problem of understanding humor, wit, or satire. See a smiley face, assume the presence of humor. Of course, there are the venerable acronyms 'lol' and its cognates (lmfao, rofl) that also became allies in the digital attempts at humor. While for many digital natives lol was known to mean "laugh out loud," there are a few cases when people mistakenly took it to mean "lots of love." I recall a pastor who used to sign emails to congregates who had suffered a tragedy with lol to indicate his warm feeling towards them. Imagine his shock when he realized what it really meant. I was there. It was quite the sight. It was also funny watching folks explain to him his error. As in rofl funny.

Exercise: Have you ever had to clear up a confusion someone had with a saying or phrase?

I have. It's wonderfully awkward, but necessary.

The ;-) is a multipurpose symbol. We can use it to indicate that we were attempting to be funny, as well indicate that we found something funny. In our now much wider worldwide web, we have a smorgasbord of available cues for indicating humor. We have enough GIF's, emoji's and emoticons to fill the sky, and even more creative keystroke combinations beyond the oft-used ;-). We have ¯_(ツ)_/¯, ☺, :-D, and :-J (tongue in cheek). There are more, but I didn't want to get into them all, nor have I the typing skills to do that easily. I simply copied the shrugging shoulders one. Like anything on the web, there's a vastness there. The keyboard gymnastics were a bit more than I cared to do. The prevalence and number of these cues shows just how important it is to make our communicative intentions clear. Without these ways to disambiguate our meaning, there would be a lot of misunderstandings. Just as we need to indicate when we're joking face-to-face, we need analogs of these behaviors in the digital environ.

As soon as people were chatting in the early chatrooms and forums over a digital medium, the need arose for a useful way to indicate one was trying to be funny, sarcastic, or satirical. The need to indicate how we were feeling to help others interpret our texts became important because of the rapidity with which we were now able to communicate. There was also another reason we needed reliable ways to indicate humor. For some reason we tend be uncharitable in our interpretations when it comes to Internet or text-based communications. Why we're apt to infer meanness rather than humor in some text is funny if you think about it. Perhaps not funny ha-ha, but strange nonetheless. It's sort of funny-sad really. I think one of the reasons that we tend to make serious or unfriendly interpretations of text is because text, rather than spoken language is much more formal. Learning to read is hard, and writing something down is seen as a serious thing to do. As I've been saying throughout, humor tends to do well in places where there are fewer constraints. The written work tends to be constrained. If you've ever had a comment or text interpreted in a negative way when you meant it as a joke or a bit of humor, then you know the importance of Poe's Law. It's imperative that you be clear that you're attempting to use humor lest someone become angry with you or perhaps worse, offended.

Even as someone who likes to use humor and has been complimented on his use of it, humor in the digital expanse takes some getting used to. There is seemingly no end to the mistakes that we can make. If you think about it, there's an obvious reason for this. It has a lot to do with how we communicate humor. Humor largely works when a typical way of interpreting some words or ideas is turned upside down, revealing the clever twist. Here's a little joke about our web habits.

> If you've ever gotten bored surfing the internet and then grabbed your phone just to see what the mini-internet has going on, you may need some help.

If you get this joke, and I sadly did, then you know quite a bit about how humor works. There's the irony, the addictive sort of behavior hopping from screen to screen indicates, and then the admission that you too need some assistance decoupling from the web. Maybe I should just wrap the book up now and encourage you not to joke and lol digitally, but rather do it with some friends outside. You should. You really should.

Exercise: Find a person you're close to as a friend, coworker, family member, and tell them a corny joke. Now have a conversation with them: at minimum a real 5-minute conversation.

Typically understanding humor in face-to-face interactions isn't difficult. We use all sorts of ways to indicate we're being funny. Researchers call these signals metalinguistic or paralinguistic cues. These are just ten cent words to identify any non-linguistic behavior that helps understand meaning from things we read or hear. Some of those metalinguistic cues are exaggerated vocal intonations and, exaggerated body language. Emoji's and GIF's are a type of these as well. They all help us understand and or communicate that the meaning of the text we're reading may be more than we might initially appreciate.

The challenge for us would-be digital humorists, is that we must find ways to add humor cues to our messages consistent with Poe's Law. It's easier to indicate humor face-to-face. Sometimes it's as easy as adding a laugh. My laughter can be an indication that we're moving into a non-serious mode of communication or that what I said should be taken as meaning something different that one might initially think. Just remember that when it comes to laughter, not all laughs are necessarily indications of humor. Some of us laugh when we're embarrassed. Sometimes we laugh to embarrass people by laughing at them. If you've ever laughed at someone while saying "yeah, right" then you know that laughter has a variety of uses beyond humor.

We need to be conscious of the fact that not everyone will be reading the text we write or content we create in the way it may be offered. While it may be perfectly obvious to us that we were being funny, or at least trying to be so, it may not be clear to the audience. As a result, you need to spend more time making your intentions known. This is different, as you know, from the easier face-to-face settings. And even then we can make mistakes.

One of the main ways we indicate that we're using humor in settings when we're in close physical proximity to one another that causes real trouble in digital/virtual environments involves using a pause. The pause helps the listener "catch up" with the joke. The pause, often accompanied by other metalinguistic cues, and the look we give helps the listener, our shift in body language, clue the audience into the fact that what we said might mean something different than what one might assume on a first pass. This pause gives the listener time to reinterpret the words so as to get the humor. Sometimes in my classes, I have to actually indicate by saying, "that was a joke" because students are often not expecting humor in a stodgy philosophy class or any college class for that matter. The role of environmental expectations is strong, and the same sorts of expectations of seriousness can be found in digital spaces related to workplaces or organizations. However useful a pause is for us in a face-to-face setting, it's not nearly as helpful in the digital environment.

Our venerable pause is not well-suited to the digital environment because instead of reinterpreting, we generally assume something else, something less friendly to communication. When we encounter an unexpected pause over a screen in a meeting our default thought is that there's been a tech issue. The bandwidth has been eaten up, processors are full, Google has shut down, etc. As a result, we start trying to troubleshoot. We are not looking for humor, we're looking for issues. That mentality is a big obstacle to laughs.

In the digital world, a pause is not indicative of humor. It's a signal that something is amiss. As a result of this predisposition we are less able to see humor when it arises. We've been trained to assume there's an issue interfering with the task at hand. As a result, we'll trot out the standard questions like "can you hear me?" "Is there a problem?" "Did Mike just get disconnected?" When you're looking for issues and to solve the problems, you tend to be singularly focused on a certain issue and less able to see the humor even if it's covered in emoji's.

Humor will be harder to express when one of the main tools sends people into trouble-shooting mode rather than levity time. Instead of responding with a smiley face emoji, we might misinterpret an exaggerated voice as someone overcompensating for a volume issue. Instead of letting the exaggerated gesticulations indicate humor, we may think there's a computer glitch, or the person doesn't realize that their camera is on, or there's a sound problem. If we can't hear them, we instinctively raise our own voices and yell. As if that really helps. Why do we think we have to speak louder when we can't hear another person?" It's odd isn't it? How my being loud solves the problem is funny when you think about it. Ah the power of everyday incongruities. Some comedians make bank on noticing these things. The show *Seinfeld* was largely based on these sorts of everyday oddities.

You may now be thinking, with all the above handwringing, that humor on the internet is fraught with issues. What with all the trolls, the mistaken interpretations, and the other issues, perhaps it should be avoided. That would be throwing the baby out with the bathwater. The digital world is just another place where humans gather and interact. If there are humans interacting, humor is certainly lurking about as well. So how can we become better at using humor in the digital space? People across a variety of web platforms can and do use humor well. How do they do it while the rest of us have difficulties? How is that YouTube and Facebook and other social media sites seem to do it so well? The answer isn't too hard to see.

One of the things you need to know is that humor on YouTube or any other platform is that those videos are tailored and sorted to be humorous. YouTube can even recommend videos that are considered humorous to you. Eventually, AI will crack a good joke. YouTube tracks your preferences and builds recommendations based on them. If the content is tagged in some way as humor and you tend to look for humorous things, then you're going to see more of them when visit the site. With techniques like sorting, hashtags, and classification, the audience, us, knows going in that the content is supposed to be funny and are thus ready and willing to laugh.

We want to find the purportedly funny things funny. You don't get that sort of audience when in your Zoom chat with the company partners or a potential new client. Again, that assumed division between work and play makes things more difficult than they need to be. When you're doing work, serious work, any non-integral interruption is not an occasion for a smile, but rather a reason to make sure nothing's wrong. It's a problem to fix.

What you've probably figured out by now is that you've got to do some prep work to let people know that you're going to use humor or that humor is acceptable. So much of what I've written about using humor begins with proper preparation. You need to set that stage a bit more. There's a technique I am sure many of you have already used to help lighten up your digital meeting presence—the virtual background. If you want to tell people that it's not all about business, that you're creative or fun-loving, there's no better way to begin than to have a fun digital background. Unless you're in a super-serious meeting, backgrounds are an easy and safe way to begin your digital use of humor. It's sort of like a fun tie or crazy socks for the Zoom crowd.

Setting the stage begins not just when you log in or enter into the digital space. Sowing the seeds of levity takes time. Some simple ways to indicate that you're being active and creative would be to sporadically change the closing of your emails to colleagues. Instead of the standard "cheers" or "I hope all is well," begin with something different. They may not read it, but they may. But if you can add in playful additions or changes in the normal digital interaction, people are going to be ready for times when you more actively use humor. One thing I've done is played around with the typical "If you have any more questions, please don't hesitate to ask." I've sometimes written "If you have any further questions, please *hesitate* to ask." For those that read carefully or pay more attention to my words, the reward is the playful little joke. It also makes the folks smile a bit and maybe be friendlier to me.

A crucial element to using and recognizing humor is you must be engaged as both a listener and speaker. If you're checking the smaller screen while you're on the meeting, if you're doing too many side chats in the chat box, you're going to miss something. Apparently the online attention span is about eight seconds. Less time than it took to read these sentences—which is probably why those YouTube ads are so short. Further, online meetings decrease our attention span and not just because there are distractions. We have to do more monitoring of the faces, the chat box, the shared screen, all while looking into the camera so as to seem as if we're looking at our audience. Online interaction is tough.

The digital space requires that we spend more time paying attention and more energy to do it. You have to look at the camera while also looking at the participants' faces in a web-meeting. Other reasons it's hard are that we can open up multiple tabs in our internet browser, we have a second browser in our pockets, and all the other distractions that exist when you're in a space that isn't a meeting space. Maybe your pet or child made a cameo. At the time of writing, amid the pandemic with five of us in my family working and schooling from home, I can hear two of my sons and wife working. It's not ideal for the concentration I need for writing. We philosophers tend to do our work alone. Being engaged in a digital space does take more investment, but that investment will pay off. If you can make digital meetings engaging, then you'll have made a huge win. While the digital world opens up a variety of possibilities and helps us deal with particular problems, it comes with its own challenges as we're all becoming aware.

If you can find ways to remain engaged, to be present as a speaker (much easier) and a listener (more difficult), you're going to find that the meetings and digitally based interactions go all the better. You may find more opportunities to use and experience humor. Furthermore, the more present you are, the more engaged you are, the more likely others will be as well. Whether you're leading the meeting, or an attendee, that sort of engagement tends to bring others along with you.

Once you've focused on your engagement approach, you need to do some other things to indicate that levity is appreciated. Start things off with a smile. Ask people how they're doing, and really mean it. Don't just accept the "fine" response we all too often give as a matter of course. Maybe instead of asking the general question, ask something specific. How was your drive in? Asking that question in an online meeting would be a funny way to start. Are you working remotely? Have you had any unwanted interruptions? Is your cat/kid popping in for a momentary levity break?

My dogs love to bark. A colleague playfully responds when her children interrupt her in a digital meeting or require attention that she needs to attend to her "interns." You know I stole that one. It's clever and effective because it acknowledges the situation and plays around with it thus making it lighter and less interruptive. That light touch allows us all to easily return to the task at hand. Whatever you do, try anything you can to get people out of rote and routine responses and get them to make their minds more present. At first it's going to feel a little stilted, but once you've set things up, it will become part of your space. Then the humor will come.

Once you're engaged, paying attention, you can now start to introduce elements of levity and humor. There are two methods of communication in the digital world. The first is via text. If you're working in this domain, emoji's, emoticons, and any of the now digital metalinguistic cues you can add to your text are crucial. You must expect that people will not understand that you're trying to use humor unless you explicitly indicate it. There's an important rule when using emoji's, emoticons, and other paralinguistic cues. They rarely if ever precede the text they're attached to. They're almost always added on at the end. And this has a lot to do with how we use humor normally.

Imagine me telling you in conversation, "Hey. This next bit is really funny." You're now expecting something funny. If you don't get it or get it and not find it funny you'll be confused. It's kind of like asking a person who's reputed to be funny to be funny right now. It feels contrived, canned, and certainly unfunny. You can't just type "Hey, this next bit is a joke." It tends to ruin the joke. An important part of humor is the spontaneity of it. We laugh when we catch the clever bits only after we've thought about it in the "wrong" way. Telling on something beforehand threatens this spontaneity. The emoticons, or whatever you're using, come after the written content preserving more of how we typically use humor. If you follow this rule of putting the emoji's or GIF's at the end, you're going to find that your digital humor is acting in ways more like how we normally communicate and thus more effective.

While it's very important to let people know you're being funny, doing it can be tough. Think again about me advertising that what comes next is going to be funny. Imagine that in as email or even in this book I was to write "Hey, this next bit is funny." Your expectations are substantially changed as a result. But if I let the conversation or the written word carry on as normal, and then at the end pull the rug out from underneath you, you then work out the humor, you recognize it, and you find it funny—if all goes to plan. If you're wanting to use more humor and have it be a tool you use well, then make sure you're avoiding too much set up, too much crafting of the space. That will feel contrived, and people will then be hesitant, they'll feel set up. If you create the conditions, if you promote humor and laughter overall, then you will find that those rugs aren't so much as pulled from under folks, they're just turned around a little bit. People will start seeing the humor for themselves.

It isn't always bad that we advertise our jokes. We can and do indicate we're attempting to be funny by telling people we're going to be telling a joke. "Hey, I heard this great joke yesterday." Though that's more the exception than the rule. If you heard someone say "a priest, a monk, and a rabbi walked into a bar. . ." you'd likely know it was a joke, since that set up is a well-known joke beginning. With written text emoji's and the rest tend to follow after the content we intend to be funny. There's research out there that supports this too. Emoticons and emoji's at the beginning tend to cause confusion. It's the equivalent of laughing at a joke before you tell it. We hate when people do that because it ruins the joke. Our expectations can't live up to their suggestions that this will be really funny.

While emoticons and such are great, I am a particular fan of GIF's and memes. The standard use of GIF's and memes is couched in humor. When you use them, your audience knows that you're using humor. They're going to expect humor, because that's the sort of content that GIF's and memes convey. You thus get to bring in with you the expectation that surrounds things like memes and GIF's, in that they're funny, and your audience is more ready to receive the humor. Again, it's all about priming and moving your audience into a space where the humor is expected and appreciated.

Another tool you can use requires a bit more time and effort. It's a sort of long game for humor. You need to advertise that humor is as acceptable in the digital space as it is in the non-digital world. Like I mentioned in the chapters on meetings and workspaces, it's crucial that you let people know that some levels of humor are appreciated. Maybe you have a "best beach" background contest for the next Zoom meeting. The next challenge gets to be chosen by the winner of that challenge. Make it a game. Winners get fantastic prizes of skipping the next themed Zoom meeting. Maybe you make sure that your emails have fun little games or comics/memes in them. What you're doing is creating an expectation in your audience that the humor is part of how you interact. The presence of humor does as much to indicate that it's acceptable in serious areas, as it does to show that you value it. This sort of approach is not nearly as odd as you may first think.

The founder and former CEO of Southwest Airlines, Herbert Kelleher, made humor an integral part of his company. From the funny flight attendants to his own interactions with staff, he and his company were well known for using humor. Clients appreciated it. Kelleher took this focus on humor and made it clear that he was about the people he worked with and the people he serviced. He famously said,

> "We will hire someone with less experience, less education, and less expertise, than someone who has more of those things and has a rotten attitude. Because we can train people. We can teach people how to lead. We can teach people how to provide customer service. But we can't change their DNA."

This quote relates directly to humor, and more importantly directly to one of the reasons that 1) humor is not used as much, and 2) why people feel so overall disengaged from their work. If we focus on the bottom line, we lose the really important factor when it comes to work: the people: the employees and customers, we serve. When we learn, as Kelleher did, to focus on people and the levity we all crave, we'll have a better organization. We'll enjoy things more. Like Kelleher, you can start to create this sort of feeling and environment. It will take a little while, but in the end, it's worth it.

Humor isn't always going to get you laughs and camaraderie. We all know that humor, like many other things can and does have a darker side. One of the more vexing issues facing anyone using humor in a digital space is that people often use humor in a variety of ways to demean, ridicule, or make fun. This sort of use is more prevalent in asynchronous sorts of content like blogs, chat discussions, or videos that can be accessed whenever, as opposed to synchronous digital engagements like a Zoom meeting, or an active real-time chat. There's a word for those who demean, ridicule, and make fun on the internet: internet trolls. For a humor apologist like me, they present a big challenge for anyone using humor in the digital space.

Let me begin this part by trying to tell you what I am not doing. I am not saying all teasing is wrong, nor is all ridicule. We tease in both prosocial and bullying ways. Ridicule has been used since the time of at least the ancient Greeks in their use of satire. In fact, the patron saint of my discipline of Western philosophy, Socrates, was the target of some rather stinging satire in Aristophanes' comedy *The Clouds*. Socrates even hung out and drank with Aristophanes and apparently did not think ill of him for the way he was lampooned. A modern term that might capture the relationship is "frenemies." Socrates at least thought the mockery was funny. There's something to be said to having thick skin.

Returning to the idea of teasing. My friends will tease me about any number of things. But they can, they're my friends. Perhaps if all they ever did was tease me I'd worry, but then we would no longer be friends. What I want you to realize is that in the digital space, things like being able to see your behavior and use that to understand what you mean, are important. But just as important to us understanding if someone is giving us a friendly tease versus a bullying one rests on what we know about the person teasing us. Are they a friend? Do I have the sort of relationship with them that permits teasing? Are they a good person? Those all play into how we judge the person as being an internet troll as opposed to a friend messing with us, or as the British like to say "giving us the piss." Having regular face-to-face access to you and not simply relying on text or content devoid of important context, makes using humor easier. The digital environment is often devoid of those things.

We have all teased and been teased, been the object of ridicule as well ridiculed others. We may have even tried to be satirical, but I am not a satirist. So the humor I use has to be different. In general, I would suggest that you find ways to use humor that has no person as a target. Try not to make fun of something that may cause someone to feel bad. If you focus on looking for incongruities in the world, not in the people in it, you're going to find some content ready made for humor.

The digital world is here to stay. It's a part of who the world we inhabit and more and more of our interactions are digitally mediated. With the pandemic we now have a strong indication of how important humor is going to be as we move ahead. Digital meetings will increase, as will our physical isolation from others. These are not happy conditions for humor. But while the initial outlook may be a bit deflating, if you take time to make humor part of your day-to-day, part of your digital expressions, not just a thing you imbibe, you can transform that digital space into a more convivial place. You can help arrest the growth of trolls, something that's desperately needed, and make sure that the vital presence of humor in your digital space and overall life remains.

CHAPTER 12

Humor and Apologies

This wouldn't be a very good book on humor and how to use it better if I didn't address those times when humor goes awry. This book has largely been about promoting the benefits of humor and how the overall lack of it in our organizational spaces hurts us. I hope that at this point you largely agree that our lives are improved when we have more humor in the world. But humor and laughter are neither inherently good nor inherently bad. Jokes can be used to educate, to promote laughter, and yes, to harm. We ridicule, make fun, and ignore the feelings and positions of others with humor. In those cases we're adding insult to the injury. We laugh at the harm done. While satire and even the occasional witty barb can be helpful, humor can be problematic when we use it as a weapon.

While it should be obvious that ridicule and making fun are generally bad, it's not always clear why. The sort of ridicule that I am talking about is different than the convivial teasing that happens among friends. It might be enough to remind us that, "if you can't say anything nice, don't say anything at all." If that does the trick, then maybe this will be the shortest chapter ever. But that's clearly not enough because humor is often used to hurt others regardless of what we may have been taught in pre-school.

One of the first things to get out there is the dangerous quality or insidious nature of using humor to ridicule. Humor and laughter are largely associated with, for lack of a better term, "good fun." So right there you get a sense of the issue. When you're laughing while you demean, you are taking pleasure by acting in ways that harm people. That's why Plato and many other thinkers worried that humor and laughter were vicious. Plato thought it was the height of immoral behavior to take delight in demeaning others. It's a moral failing to laugh at the misfortune or bad behavior of others. You're literally enjoying the debasement of others. For him it was literally grotesque. That can't be good. While this sort of view of humor is largely out of favor (it's called the Superiority Theory—and we briefly mentioned it back in chapter 4), if you look at how we sometimes use humor, it's supported.

 Exercise: Can you think of a time when you ridiculed or made fun of someone? Was it a friendly tease or was it something more? How do you know the difference?

As I've said, the first thing to notice when you're using humor—and this is not an original insight—is to avoid ridicule. This is especially important in organizational spaces where there are hierarchies and people can be harmed in a variety of ways by the errant quip. If I am a manager and I make a joke about one of my employee's issues, that act has far more negative repercussions than you might think. Other employees might infer from my actions I have said ridicule is ok here. They may also use that joke as a starting ground to make fun of that same employee. An environment where there is a lot of bullying and teasing going on is not a good one. It makes all involved less engaged and productive. Many of us have experienced bullying in the past and have felt the negative effects of it.

The example above is another easy one to get your head around. It's easy to identify the one being harmed and the harmful behavior. If I make fun of you, and mean to do harm it's much easier to see the bad outcome. That sort of joking and teasing is bad enough and has a number of issues with its use. But there are other ways to demean and ridicule that are worse. One that's the most insidious and does more irreparable harm comes when the jokers or teasers are using the humor in what they think is a prosocial as opposed to bullying way. Someone thinks he or she is being funny but is harming others in the process.

Let me give you an example from my own experience. My oldest son is gay. He came out to us when he was fourteen. It wasn't easy. He started by coming out to his mother, and it took a few months for him to discuss it with me. In fact, I had to approach him and let him know that I knew. If I hadn't come forward, I may still not "know." Sexual orientation is still a difficult topic, and being a teenager with all the attendant issues that age brings just made dealing with it and us all the more difficult. For me, his being gay was and is a non-issue. In dealing with his being gay, I used humor so we could open up lines of communication.

Shortly after we first discussed his orientation, I wanted him to know that it wasn't an issue. I told him about the first time I was hit on by a gay man, how awkwardly I handled it, and how I had learned from a friend that being hit on was a compliment and clearly not something to worry about. It wasn't a threat to my sexuality. That was a hugely helpful piece of advice. I made a little fun of myself, and hoped that in doing so it would help him to relax. (One of the benefits of self-deprecatory humor) It seemed to work. Some time later we were picking up his brother from soccer practice and there were a bunch of soccer players all hanging around and I decided to mess with my son a bit. I proceeded to ask him which of these young men he found attractive. I think I said, "So what's your type?" He was immediately uncomfortable. So of course I did more and more of it. It was fun to tease him. He got it, but at a point I knew to stop. There's a point when even friendly, good-natured teasing can go too far. If you tend to use this sort of approach, be attentive.

It's not as if I just started teasing him around issues of his sexuality. My behavior as the father set an expectation. We routinely used humor to deal with issues. And like any family, we have issues. That's just life. I had already established that we could be sarcastic and tease. But however much I used teasing and humor, no matter how well-intentioned my jokes and teases might have been, it runs the risk of doing exactly what I don't want to happen. I could hurt my son.

The reason for this is that the subject matter of the teases touches on sexuality and this can be a deeply sensitive subject as it clearly was for him. While I may only mean to tease and to play, there is something that no amount of teasing or friendly ribbing can resolve. It's still the case that in the USA, even after the landmark *Obergefell* case that guarantees the right to same-sex marriage, being gay is still an issue for some. Some view it as a sin and it can, in certain parts of the world, carry the penalty of imprisonment or death. It is certainly better now, but it's not as if he doesn't face issues of discrimination. I am teasing him on an issue that is difficult given the current state of our society.

So how can my humorous treatment of his being gay—my little teases here and there—be a problem for him? Because no one makes fun of me, nor are there a suite of jokes that people can dip into to tease me for being a heterosexual male. Further, I am a white, heterosexual male. To borrow the words of the talented folksinger Utah Phillips, I was born armed to the teeth with privilege. I don't ever get made fun of for being heterosexual. Sure, there is the word "breeder" that is sometimes used by gay people to refer to heterosexuals, but I've never felt threatened or harmed by its use. In fact, I think it's pretty clever. The same isn't true for the insults and "teasing" slang terms hurled at my son.

When I tease my son about being "gay" or use that word in such a way as to tease him, I am dipping into a world that is sometimes hostile to him for being gay. A hostility I never feel for being straight. He knows that I don't mean it in a bad way. But still the specter that that word has, all that it entails both good and ill, relates to him in ways I don't understand as he does. As the one using the humor, as the one sitting in a position of authority, his father, I need to be more aware of this. I can't wait for him to tell me he's feeling uncomfortable. I need to pay attention to him. Because even if I am joking, that he's hurt at times or feels discomfort, is a result quite opposite to what I want when I use humor. As the one initiating the humor I've a responsibility to pay attention to what it does.

This example can easily be changed to fit issues of race, sex, class, and ethnicity, among others. I am not saying all such humor is wrong and to be avoided. There is some brilliant satire that uses all of the above. I have joked with my friends based on issues of gender, sexual orientation, etc. And no, not all of my friends are white cis males. Sometimes only friends can joke along such lines. But when we're inhabiting organizational spaces, we need to be aware of all of these markers, of the assumed formality of the space, and how individuals relate not just within the organization but also within the broader cultural context. Those multiple layers of contexts and markers give us a shifting ground from which to judge our humor. It's not easy.

Returning to my son, imagine the following situation. Philosophers love to imagine things by the way. I claim that I am okay with my son's orientation. I try to make him feel welcome and safe. I am even convinced that I have no issues with his being gay. But let's imagine that my jokes about him being gay are pretty frequent. If you heard me making jokes, teasing, and poking fun at gay people on a regular basis, if it was daily, you might begin to wonder if I were really as "cool with it" as I claim. And you wouldn't be wrong. We often use humor as a way to express our anger, discomfort, or dislike of certain things without actually admitting it. In this hypothetical situation, the jokes early on seemed like I was using the humor to show I was fine with the situation, but they were actually a cover for my discomfort: a defense mechanism. Instead of using the jokes as friendly humor, I am, again, in this situation, allowing the jokes to release my hostilities.

To extend this a bit further, imagine that my son gets annoyed with my constant joking and he's fed up. He comes to me and says something like "Enough!" He's done that for other things because, you know, parents can be a bit extra at times. I can tell he's annoyed, but I just look at him and say

"I was just joking. Quit being so sensitive." Let's call this the "just joking" defense. It's a ploy used by politicians, radio hosts, celebrities, and pretty much anyone who's ever been called on a joke ever since people started making jokes. This response commits a number of blunders. First off it deflects responsibility. My son calls me out on something I said. He finds it hurtful and I just respond telling him he's wrong. He didn't ask for the joke or invite me to make a funny comment. I am the one who started the ball rolling as it were. When someone does a thing on their own, it's typically the case that they're responsible for what it does. It's a basic premise behind the idea of responsibility. The words were mine, said by me to my son, and I did so on purpose. I can't just step back from them because they're an attempt at humor.

That's just the beginning of the disingenuousness of the just joking defense. When I point out that he's being too sensitive, I am immediately dismissing his response by saying something's wrong with him, not me. Again, I started all this, so I am foisting more onto the victim here. It's a total and absolute dodge. It's also a dodge that happens to tap into a stereotype of gay males being "too sensitive" or feminine. So not only am I avoiding taking any sort of responsibility for what I say, I am both demeaning and dismissing any of my son's feelings. Imagine if your friend, coworker, or boss treated your complaints in a way that just ignored the complaint and/ or said that you were wrong for even bringing it up. The atmosphere from then on out would be much worse. That's what the just joking defense can and often does.

There are two further things to explore here. What if it turns out that I was, in fact, only joking? Does making a joke absolve me from any responsibility? It seems funny to think that just because a person is joking it thereby makes them less responsible for what their words do, right? If we made the joke, we own it some way. One way to deal with this situation is to acknowledge the target's response however it is offered. Jokes can and do go awry. If I were to tell my son that I understand his response and then promise to be more sensitive to his feelings as I joke in the future, that's a great thing. I am not hiding behind the humor, I am acknowledging his response to it and my change in behavior acknowledges him as a person, as an individual (not a means to my comedy). This doesn't mean I can't find the joke funny, or that I am wrong for finding it funny. It means that I am aware that he doesn't find it funny, and worse still, he is offended by it. That I recognize that, is important. Recognizing this in the organizational space, or in your personal life will increase the strength of those relationships.

The second way the just joking defense runs afoul is that what if, as I mentioned earlier, I am really not just joking? What if I am using the humor as a proxy for my disagreement with certain things? We can and do use humor to hide our dislike of things. Think of when we use sarcasm or make fun. Instead of coming out and saying "I don't like X" I make snide or snarky comments or jokes. Then the just joking defense is even worse. I am here using the joke to be mean, to make fun of and ridicule and when called on for precisely that, because the person targeted feels hurt, I immediately shift all blame and focus away from me—the person actively playing the part of the bully. That's simply and literally adding insult to injury. Any relationship where that's a baseline—where one person attempts to hurt another and then says that the person hurt is wrong for pointing out how hurtful the words are—is pretty much awful. It seems like an abusive relationship. Clearly we want to avoid using humor that promotes abuse.

It's not as if any time someone uses a joke and another person gets offended that there was some deep sin committed. Sometimes it's a misunderstanding of intent. My son thinks I am making fun of him rather than me sharing a joke. What the actual responsibility of any joke teller has when using humor depends on a vast number of things. Comedians and satirists are clearly making fun with an end goal, so they can and often are expected to cause some level of offense. But we're not often in the role of satirist, even if our organizations could use some institutional satirists. There's a lot more that could be said on this topic, but that's probably best left to a paper in ethical theory and not this book. But do remember, the world is a complex place, and we never know all we can about a person. If you think about our Humor as a House allegory, you will probably do just fine. Be friendly until you get your foot in the door and continue to use gentle humor until you know the person well and are joking around the kitchen table.

Exercise: Have you ever used humor as a way to "safely" complain about things?

I am not here to say that any humor or jokes that rely on topics of race, sexual orientation, ethnicity, and gender are forbidden. If that were the case we would be without some of the greatest satire and humor in the world. Satire like the kind found in *Blazing Saddles,* or The Race Draft sketch from *Chappelle Show* are two great examples. In fact, the exchange between my assistant director and me from chapter 10 is clear evidence that such humor is great. But there are some rules you can use to help use humor that touches on these topics.

The first one is to understand the difference between what is sometimes called "punching up" and "punching down." The idea here is that humor that punches up, that is, it's humor coming from someone lower in the organizational hierarchy and targeting someone or something higher up, is generally more acceptable. If my son makes fun of me by calling me a "boomer," that's punching up. If I use a slang/slur term common often used to refer to gay men toward him I'm punching down. When you're thinking of using a joke that may demean, then first figure out whether you're punching up or down. Try to be cognizant of not only your role and place in the organization but also the role you occupy in the wider society. Those are important too. Given my own position in our social order, I may be punching down more than I punch up. Generally, avoid punching down. Punching up is much better. But also remember that what may be punching up in one context may be seen as punching down in another. It's not always easy to know so it will take some practice. But if you're paying more attention to these sorts of issues, you are necessarily more engaged and will find more ways to use humor effectively.

The idea of punching up/down is a relatively modern one. For instance, Aristotle said that a person of high social stature should never worry about jokes made by people from a lower social status. Literally, those people are beneath them and needn't be worried about. The notion of a court jester or the "fool" from the medieval period is clearly a form of punching down. The point of the jester was to be laughed at. Satirists from Jonathan Swift to the creators of *South Park* punch up, down, left, right, forward and backward. Their punches spare no one. This idea of refraining from punching down is new and has had some interesting results in modern stand-up comedy. Some stand-up that was once seen as funny is now seen as being in poor taste. I am not interested in taking a position on things like "cancel culture" or "political correctness" in this book. It's not the place for it. But what you the reader need to be aware of is that how we evaluate and respond to humor, to how comedy is influenced in a number of ways by our current sociocultural environment. Since humor is a social activity, these influences are unavoidable and as such, knowing them will help you do humor better.

It's important, particularly if you're a leader of any sort, that you encourage people to seek you out when they find certain forms of humor inappropriate. There's nothing particularly innovative here. Just let people know that you are open to people discussing issues they may have with humor as it may happen in your organization. In the same way that humor encourages engagement, this request for feedback is also a way to help people be engaged by showing that you value engagement. These feedback loops are crucial for all involved.

The final portion of this chapter concerns apology as a way to address humor gone awry. When I give talks to groups on humor, it doesn't take long for people to ask what to do when a joke or an attempt at humor goes awry. I take a moment then talk about apology. I then apologize for not giving them something more groundbreaking. It feels like I am letting them down, but I am not. An apology is still the best way to address those times when our humor has consequences beyond what we were expecting. The first thing to note is that your apology has to be meaningful and authentic.

Exercise: Have you ever heard someone apologize by saying "I am sorry that my words caused you harm?" or something like" it? Do you think that's a good apology? Have you ever done it? I have.

Too often we hear politicians, public officials, and others use language like this and offer a non-apology. One of the reasons it's so annoying is that it borrows the language of an apology but doesn't apologize. It looks like an apology, smells like one, but isn't one. Its entire point is to get the apologizer out of trouble without actually doing what's expected of an apology. All the reward with no actual work.

An apology isn't just a scripted set of words. It's a sort of promise. When I apologize to someone, it's not just that I am sorry for what I did. Yes, that's a big part of it. Beyond the apology, or perhaps within any good apology, I am also recognizing that what I did is something that could have hurt someone. When I use the faux apology, I am not really recognizing that I caused harm. In saying, "I am sorry if my words offended" I am taking no responsibility. Just like the "just joking defense" we are seeking to escape responsibility. It was either the words that harmed you or you taking offense to the words. In either case, I am not really to blame here. At worst, I just chose the wrong words. I wasn't meaning to hurt anyone. You're just being too sensitive.

The problem with that is we need to be aware that our words' effects outstrip the meaning intended. I am also, again whether I mean to or not, able to hurt others by what I say even if I meant not to, even if I meant to have fun or just joke around. My cavalier joking with my sons, partner, colleagues, or friends might have caused them pain at times, regardless of my intent. If my "apology" effectively dismisses any complaint or concern from another that will create situations where people are not well respected, it could fracture the relationship further. This is corrosive to a healthy environment.

Apologies also do more than offer up a means to acknowledge that a wrong was done. If they're sincere, they're also promises. It's a promise to avoid such behavior in the future. When I apologize to my friend for ignoring them, their feelings, their invitations, if I don't then start paying attention to their invites, then my apology has done a lot less than we expected. It's actually worse than no apology at all because the apology was offered insincerely. It exacerbates the fracture. I am trying to buy you off with counterfeit words. Apologies are more than words, they're social acts. These acts are important ways we maintain our relationships in the same way that humor does.

So remember that when you're apologizing you need to be sincere. Don't dodge issues, especially if you're in a leadership role. That sets a bad precedent. Further, you need to be on the lookout that the humor you're using doesn't have any untoward effects, intended or not. You made the joke, you can't just give over responsibility. We are trained, in part by the actions of comedians and humorists, that jokes and such are special, and for them they are. But remember, you're not a comedian, you're not doing art or performance.

Humorists, satirists, comedians, even the clown occupy a special place in our societies. They are expected to poke fun at things, cross boundaries, push the line of appropriateness. That's part of the reason we pay money to go to comedy clubs, watch shows, or read their work. They are allowed to broach topics that we cannot in our everyday lives. They have a role and fill it. As a regular person making a joke here or there, or making the funny comment at work or at home, you're just being funny. There's no marquee outside your house telling people you're headlining tonight's edition of dinner chat. The only place you're headlining is wherever you happen to be, and that's not a comedy club or humor special on Netflix. As a result of these different social spaces, your humor is going to be bound more by the general rules we use to guide our normal interactions. Not being a jerk is one of them. Don't be a jerk when you use humor.

As we close this chapter, remember, humor is a great thing. But it, like so much else, can be problematic in its use. Even when we've the best intentions. There are things we need to be mindful of with our use of humor, and if we are, our humor can be all the more effective. It can bring more people together and encourage more engagement. Even when the humor goes wrong, we can look at that situation as a way to increase our engagement. When we really take the time to apologize, to understand the other person, we are engaging them in a similarly deep way like we do when we use humor. You can even throw in a little self-deprecatory humor when you apologize by mocking your own insensitivity or clumsiness. In both apology and humor we are reaching out and connecting with important parts of the person. When we do that, we strengthen our relationships and are the better for it.

Exercise: This was a pretty heavy chapter, so take a moment (or a bunch of moments) and relax a bit. Think about the things we covered, or don't. Just don't completely forget them. As you learn to use humor, you also learn more about when and how it fails. Knowledge doesn't always make things easier or settled. Sometimes as we learn, we realize how much we don't know. It keeps academics like me in business.

CHAPTER 13

He Who Laughs Lasts: Concluding Thoughts

The number thirteen is my lucky number, so it felt right to end the book here. Mark Twain once wrote, "The human race has only one really effective weapon, and that is laughter. The moment it arises, all your irritations and resentments slip away and the sunny spirit takes their place." A different famous quote about success starts by telling us that one of the foremost indicators of success is "To laugh often and much." We all know how valuable laughter, humor, and mirth are not just for feeling good. It helps us face the difficulties we must with that oft missing sunny spirit. Let's be honest, if you've followed along this far, you know humor and laughter are important parts of a rich and impactful life. It's now on you to put into practice some of the things you've learned so far.

 Final(ish) Exercise: Take a moment and think of three things you've learned from this book that you want to do or try to increase humor in your day-to-day life. How will you accomplish these things?

With that, we now turn towards the conclusion of this book. Hopefully this ending represents a new beginning for you. The beginning of a path to find more ways to use humor in your life. Whether you find ways to increase the levity in your own life, or those around you, your family, and yes your organizational space, my main wish is that this book brought a smile to your face. If it encourages you to bring more laughter, humor, and mirth into the wider world, that's great too. The world is awful short on smiles, laughter, and mirth. It's up to us to change that.

We have covered a lot of ground in this book. We've gone over the basics of humor as a cognitive act and understood that incongruity is one of the best explanations of humor. We've looked at how humor is important to our health both mental and physical. We've learned how humor is important in leadership. We also covered a little allegory comparing using humor to being invited into a house and using that as a guide to understand what sorts of humor we can use and when. We've thought a bit about humor in organizational spaces like meetings and the digital environment. We've even talked about humor as an educational tool. Have we covered all that's important and relevant about humor? Not even close. I have more books, blogs, and articles to write. It's nice to have some job security. But what we have covered is more than enough to get you going to effectively bring humor into your world.

I've spent a lot of hours researching, writing, and talking about humor. Much of my success professionally and personally is due, directly or indirectly, to humor. People smile when I tell them what I research, even after they've heard I'm a philosophy professor. It's not hard to talk with folks about humor. From pleasant conversations with friends, heated discussions with colleagues, and even arguments, humor is an important part of how I work. While my professional interests may lend themselves to allowing me to use humor a bit more here and there, nowhere is it written in the book of life that we shouldn't be using humor and being on the lookout for it. There's far too much evidence that humor and laughter are beneficial. But just don't look at what humor can get you. Humor can be of benefit to those you work with: to those you love. Humor has a beautiful ability to make you interact in pleasant ways with those around you. When you do, you enrich not just yourself, but also those in your company.

There are a lot of people that I have to thank for this project coming to fruition. Books, projects, or any sort of life are not built without help, lots of it. I am no different. There are many I should thank, but only so many words up to the task. I have to thank my mother for giving me my sense of humor. It was her irreverence and exposing me to movies like *Airplane!* that pushed me to explore humor as I did. While I am handing out gratitude, I also have to thank my wife and partner who met me while I was in graduate school making no money and in a profession that wasn't likely to usher in financial wealth. At least I could dance. Oh, and apparently she liked my sense of humor. My three boys deserve mention. They help to keep levity alive in our home. Of course I would be remiss if I didn't mention all the teachers, colleagues, friends and associates that have helped me on my journey these past years. Some pushed me hard (hat tip to Dr. R. Smith) and others were constant sources of encouragement (Prof. J. Bickle). I've been blessed with gracious and intelligent colleagues (Dr. S. Kelly, Dr. Galen Foresman, to name only a couple) who have helped me by listening to my thoughts and helping me work through them. If it weren't for all these people and more, I don't get the chance write this book or any of the other things I am blessed to do. I need to thank bowl carver, and all around great artist, David Fisher, for providing the design for the mirth-man face you've been seeing through the book. Finally, the reviewers and editors (John B.) who read through early drafts deserve much thanks as does a former student Matt M. for the copy edits. Whatever errors remain, are mine. I'm both lucky and blessed to get to talk about laughter, smiles, and mirth. Those blessings only increase if by writing this book it helps to bring these things into your life dear reader.

But the most important person to thank at this point is you, the reader. You've made your way through this book, you've done some of the exercises. Hopefully you've laughed and smiled at some of the content. You're the person that has put in the time, and yes the work, to think more about using humor, about how you might do it better. That's the takeaway from this book. I encourage you to go out and take some time to practice humor. Pick one area of your life and start there. Think small, and make subtle changes. Maybe you want to start the day with a challenge to find five incongruities throughout the day. Maybe you promise to begin each day by watching a funny video. Maybe you decide to take up laughter yoga. Whatever it is, do what you have found most interesting and brings a smile to your face. Your days will become brighter.

If you would like to know more about me and my work you can visit my author page by searching Michael K. Cundall Jr. or visit my website www.mirthmanagement.co. I am available to give talks to organizations, keynote speeches, consulting, and if you're interested, a philosophy class. Oh, I also love teaching bowl and spoon carving.

I wish you success in your journey to increasing laughs, humor, and mirth. Hopefully we can all bring more smiles to the world.

Mike Cundall, December 2020
This is my Pandemic Project.

About the Author

M ike Cundall is a philosophy professor, humor scholar, father, and sometimes woodworker. He's been studying and writing on humor for the past 20 years. His company, Mirth Management (www.mirthman-agement.co) focuses on helping people and organizations increase engagement, enjoyment, and overall improve their quality of life by helping folks unlock the power of humor. He got his undergraduate degree at the University of Kentucky, and his graduate degree from the University of Cincinnati. He is married and has three boys, two dogs, and a cat. When not writing or reading about humor he can be found carving bowls and spoons or doing Aikido. He also likes pocketwatches.

APPENDIX 1

More Playbook Activities

Find Your Funny

So let's get started. Take a moment, or several moments, and write down a list of things that you find funny. Think of jokes, movies, or comedies, YouTube videos, or memes, that you find funny. Write them down. It's even better when you have things that you continue to find funny over time. So that's our first activity: Find Your Funny. If you can, glue in pictures, paper clip them, find a way to make a written link to some Internet content so you'll remember. Write down little stories from your life that were funny or brought a smile to your face. Reflect a bit on why you like them so. Are there any commonalities to what you find funny? Is there a type of humor you're drawn to? I love good Dad jokes and am particularly fun witty retorts. I rarely get to be witty in my retorts. I tend to think of good zingers long after the fact. But they are still funny.

Don't think of this as an assignment. Think of it as an exploration. It's a chance for you to explore your world of humor. You may find other things out there that you hadn't recalled initially. Ask your friends as to what they find funny maybe. Ask people close to you, maybe a partner or friend, if they notice anything about the humor you tend to use. You may find some interesting things about yourself. As you review and add to the list, are there categories of humor that pop out? Do you tend toward slapstick humor or do you like satire? Do you prefer comics who are deadpan or the more animated one? Don't put a valuation on the humor you like. Don't judge yourself to be a bad humorist because you like good old bathroom humor or fart jokes. Just lay out what you find funny. And when you're done, celebrate that list. Be on the look-out for other funny things. I think you'll find that there's more things out there that are funny than you initially thought.

- Movies

  - » I love *Airplane! Spaceballs!, Friday,* and others. You can see I like spoof movies.

- YouTube videos

  - » These are a bit trickier. I tend not to watch humor videos on YouTube. But the shampoo prank gets me every time.

- Comedy shows

  - » Huge fan of *Chappelle Show, Rick and Morty, It's Always Sunny in Philadelphia.*

- Jokes

  - » I did a stand up class, and writing jokes is a lot harder than I thought. But like anything else, it's a skill that gets better with practice.

- Stories
- Witty Comebacks
- Sarcastic Remarks
- Category of 'Miscellaneous Funny Things That Don't Fit Under a Category'

Beg, Borrow, and Steal

I make no apologies for stealing, remembering, and using other people's jokes and humor. It's really no different than sharing a joke you heard. You probably didn't make it up, but you found it funny. So why restrict yourself to humor that you didn't come up with? If you find it funny then share it. But more importantly remember it and use it again and again. You will find yourself around new and different people and those jokes will still be useful. While my partner knows many of my jokes and my sense of humor, other people don't. And remember, I may not find something you think hilarious funny, but in general, I do appreciate that people find such enjoyment.

Years ago I heard a friend of my brother's call out to some folks as they were leaving a party, "Drive fast. Take chances." I thought it was a clever little play on our typical send-off of "take care." I have kept that little phrase in my mental back pocket for years and it still does well. Of course my wife will also sarcastically mouth the words as I say them, but hey, it still gets some mileage. Good jokes, good little turns of phrase, or bits of wit can be cherished, held onto, and used over and again. I encourage you to be on the lookout for things you find funny that other's do. Then think how you might take that bit of wit and bring into your life.

Comedians and comedies are great sources of inspiration to use for humor in our organizations. Entire TV shows are based on office oddities and the workplace. *The Office, Office Space*, and many others. I heard a comedian making fun of some of the phrases we tend to use. In this bit he was focusing on the "It's always the last place you look." The comedian rightly points out that it has to be the last place you look. Because if you kept looking after you found it, well then you're insane. I love to complain about the ubiquitous saying: "It is what it is." That statement is so annoying. Whatever anything is, it has to be what it is. If it wasn't, it wouldn't be.

These are just some of the places and spaces I mine for humor. When my philosophy class is getting a bit dull, I will point out these oddities of language. It does just the right amount of waking up to keep people focused.

My student's joke about a thermos

I was teaching my first seminar class on humor at my first university, Arkansas State University, and towards the end we talks about jokes and as a way to apply some of what we had learned about how humor worked, I asked them to make a joke about something that was near them or perhaps in their backpack. Yes, jokes about laptops, notebooks, and pens do not abound nor is there anything particularly "funny" about them, so my students were struggling. One student was staring intently at his things and as I came to him, he just sort of impatiently waived me off and said, "Come back to me in like five minutes." He never even looked up. But a few minutes later he said, "I got it." The joke he laid out was great for on the spot. He chose his thermos as the subject of his joke and it went something like this.

"So a thermos walks into a bar and goes up to the bartender and says, give me a shot. He takes the cup off his head, and unscrews his lid, setting them both on the bar." All the while my student is acting out what the thermos is doing. "The thermos tells the bartender to pour the shot into his cup and proceeds to pour the shot into himself-the thermos. He orders another shot, then another, then another. All drinking them in the same way. The bartender starts to get a little worried and says to the thermos, "Hey man, don't you need to slow down?!" The thermos responds, "Nah, I'm good. I'm about half loaded and I'm about to get screwed!" As my student is saying this last part he's showing the thermos screwing his cap back on his head. It wasn't a laugh out loud joke. Hell, it might not ever be good for a comedy club but that was a damn good joke given the conditions. Read it again and try and act it out. It is so very clever. I wish I remembered that student's name.

Funny Notetaking: Funny Things Others Have Done

What are some of the funny things you've heard others say or do? Could you emulate them or use their content? Where could you do such things? Write down four to six witticisms you particularly like. Now name two to three places where you could use those jokes or humor. Can you promise me to try at least like two of them?

Playbook Activity: Everyday Incongruities

1. Take three to four days next week and write down three to four incongruities you see or notice.

   i. One thing I used to do was wet my toothbrush before I placed toothpaste on it and then again after. Why double the effort and waste water, I mean I do love my teeth, and my dentist didn't notice a change.

   ii. When students say, "Can I ask you a question?" I often respond "You just did." Other possible responses are "I'll let you ask two." Or "It seems like you can." Those always bring a little moment of levity.

2. Name some everyday absurdities—What is one of the cleverest bits you've ever seen?

   » Mt. Cleverest

   » Sillygisms

   » My middle son as a baby was a pretty hefty kid—cankles and all. I used call him "The Fatterhorn" or "Cape Fateras"

3. What are some of the oddest things you've seen in your work (emails)?

   i. Play around with them—is there a fun, non-mocking joke

   ii. Make a satirical work email post

   iii. Onboarding made easy (*Spongebob* Season 3 Episode 10b "Eager McBeaver")

4. *Humorous Environmental Upgrades*

   i. Googly Eyes at the ready. Put googly eyes on signs, pictures, or relatively appropriate objects in your organization. Make sure the adhesive isn't likely to cause damage.

   ii. Laugh Board—keep these appropriate. Fun, lighthearted and playful

      ¤ Funny comics

      ¤ Funny workplace signs/warnings

      ¤ Funny pics

5. *Meetings Are Fun—ways to add levity to meetings*

   » Catch phrase count. How many times have we used "circle back" and my least favorite "think outside the box?" Do this one in your head.

   » Send out an agenda with a simple crossword puzzle with answers from the agenda

   » Have folks sign in with their nickname/for Zoom meetings in a regular group

   » Where am I? Background quiz for one member of a Zoom meeting at the start of each meeting.

6. *Make "Best Rejections" Board.*

   » Some jobs have rejection as a daily event. Sales, being an author, dating. I had an Army recruiter tell me how hard it was on some new recruiters, folks used to success, who came in and had to deal with the high levels of rejection that recruiters get. I suggested that they create a poster board where all the recruiters could post the best rejection they experienced that month or week. Put them all up and at the end of the month have everyone read theirs, tell the story, and then vote on who had the worst one. The winner could get a gift card, or maybe the rotating worst rejection trophy. Everyone can share a laugh and commiserate. This is a great team-building exercise.

    ¤   Fair warning. I wouldn't have this be a virtual thing. Make sure that the entries are thrown away. People might get the wrong idea.

7. *Best/Funniest Email*

    »   We all make mistakes. What's the best error someone in the team has had? I worked at a restaurant called Dudley's and they gave out the Dudley Duck for the best mistake or screw up. I was in the running for a couple of years. Never won. But it was a fun bonding experience and to my recollection, no one was embarrassed. We all have off days. It's laughing at them with our friends that make it more tolerable. It also helps us to be more resilient.

APPENDIX 2

Further Reading

For those interested in reading more, I have listed some books and other sources. Some are easier reads and some are more academic in nature. I've read all of them, and many of them I own. Some of these may be to your liking and others less so, but all the books are interesting. Use this list as a starting point for your further reading. Take it in whatever direction you'd like. Happy hunting for more humor.

- *The Psychology of Humor* by Rod Martin. (textbook)
- *Comic Relief* by John Morreall
- *The Mirth of Nations* by Christie Davies
- *Jokes: Philosophical Thoughts on Laughing Matters* by Ted Cohen (this book was highly influential)
- *Using Humor to Maximize Living* by Mary Kay Morrison
- *Laughter* by Robert Provine (classic text in the field)
- *Between Heaven and Mirth* by James Martin, SJ
- *Creative Humor at Work* by Sandra Meggert
- *Anatomy of an Illness: As Perceived by the Patient* by Norman Cousins
- *Internet Encyclopedia of Philosophy entry on humor https://plato.stanford.edu/entries/humor/#pagetopright*